Harold P. Simonson earned a B. Phil. in divinity from the University of Saint Andrews, Scotland, and a Ph.D. in English from Northwestern University. Currently a professor of English at the University of Washington, he is chiefly interested in Puritan, immigrant, Middle West, and Western frontier writers. His books include *Zona Gale, Francis Grierson, The Closed Frontier,* and *Jonathan Edwards.*

W9-CWV-073

Radical Discontinuities

Radical Discontinuities

American Romanticism and Christian Consciousness

Harold P. Simonson

Rutherford • Madison • Teaneck
Fairleigh Dickinson University Press
London and Toronto: Associated University Presses

© 1983 by Associated University Presses, Inc.

PS
169
. R6
S 57
1983

Associated University Presses, Inc.
4 Cornwall Drive
East Brunswick, NJ 08816

Associated University Presses Ltd
27 Chancery Lane
London WC2A 1NF, England

Associated University Presses
2133 Royal Windsor Drive
Unit 1
Mississauga, Ontario
Canada L5J 1K5

Library of Congress Cataloging in Publication Data

Simonson, Harold Peter, 1926–
    Radical discontinuities.

    Bibliography: p.
    Includes index.
    1. American literature—History and criticism.
2. Romanticism—United States.   3. Christianity and
literature.   I. Title.
PS169.R6S57   1983   810'.9'145   81-72051
ISBN 0-8386-3159-2

Printed in the United States of America

To Carolyn

Contents

Introduction

To take up such formidable topics as Romanticism and Christian consciousness seems to belie at the outset any avowed modesty. Therefore, I must at once claim my investigation to be a modest one, even though I am emboldened to juxtapose these two vast and influential themes. My effort here is not to reconcile them but to keep them apart, to show how they stand in opposition to each other. A far more prodigious effort than what I have undertaken might send an investigator back through two millennia to trace the separateness, while taking into account the many arguments denying it. Such an effort might also involve one in discriminating among the shifting emphases associated with each tradition and making evident that no single Romantic or Christian consciousness exists as a tidy entity. I have limited my own study to the American scene and, more specifically, to the divided streams of Puritan and Romantic thought, while being aware that even within these restrictions the multiple and elusive configurations make the task of fixing the two traditions difficult.

Nevertheless, I argue for their radical distinctiveness while also seeing them both in metaphysical terms. Both traditions ask questions about God, self, nature, and community. Both presuppose human consciousness and both establish a theory of knowledge. Significant for my purpose is that both also serve as respective critiques of each other. What such terms as *genius, imagination, creativity, freedom,* and *beauty* mean in one tradition take on radically different meanings in the other. For example, to ask as a Romanticist, "In what way is imagination true?" may summon the great voices to answer, "Imagination is the very vessel by which divinity passes into humanity." The Christian, on the other hand, may only say, "Very fine, very exciting, very noble—but as the truth it really will not do!" Yet in Romantic thought such terms as *genius* and *imagination* constitute its groundwork; other ones like *sin, grace, regeneration, incarnation*—foundational in orthodox Christian theology—are given secular or, at best, mythological meaning but otherwise carry lesser importance in the Romantic view of human nature and destiny.

To extrapolate the example of imagination, orthodox Christianity that included Puritanism harbored serious distrust toward imagination's idolatrous potential. Not only might imagination lead one astray in interpreting scripture, nature, and history, but its power might also tempt one to regard human creativeness as akin to God's and, in the end, to believe the two to be one and the same. Puritan distrust of imagination extended to the beauties of the senses, including works of art, even while a rich and sensuous imagery often marked Puritan language. Nevertheless, the Puritans insisted their sermons were not works of art but means designed to initiate and support religious experience through the exegesis of the scripture, explication of Christian doctrine, and exposition of doctrinal application in one's daily life. Primacy was given to faith, not to imagination, and to the regeneration of a sinful heart that otherwise stood in natural antipathy to God's will. Whereas a later Romanticism attributed to imagination the power to unify the subjective "I" and the objective "it," to recreate nature or the "it" as an organic extension of one's own creative mind, so that the Romantic seer might ultimately say, "I am that object"—that tower, that volcano, that fowl—"all are Ahab," a Christian consciousness, by contrast, would insist that true creativeness belongs only to God, that human creativity has grandeur only as a reflection of a greater glory, and that a radical discontinuity separates the "I am" spoken by finite man and the "I AM THAT I AM" (Exod. 3:14) spoken by the God of Abraham, Isaac, and Jacob.

Because dichotomies tend to be reductionistic, a certain

risk inevitably accompanies one's efforts to structure a thesis based upon them. Contrasting faith and imagination implies an opposition not only radical but absolute. The same can be said for other distinctions such as the sacred and the profane, revelation and vision, scripture and art, God and man. Each set of terms proposes a collision of mutually exclusive contexts. These absolutist terms, however, may blur and overlap when one thinks about the doctrine of the Incarnation, or of how much literary art there is in Hebrew and Christian scripture, or of how rituals of consecration make profane things holy. As for the Bible, any reader knows that religion has a profound alliance with poetry and that scripture aims to do more than support law and doctrine. From the side of art, certain contemporary critics like Murray Krieger and Paul de Man speak of poetry as the incarnate word, and from the theological side Paul Tillich and the earlier Horace Bushnell did the same. In his "Preliminary Dissertation on the Nature of Language" in *God in Christ* (Hartford: Brown and Parsons, 1849) Bushnell argued that "all words are in fact only incarnations—forms that somehow shape the formless, and earthen vessels containing or not containing mysteries transcending their corporeal order. Whether the mystical element is in the word or the word in the mystery, either would seem to bridge the dialectic, much as the divine Logos weaves into nature types or images that seem to have an inscrutable relation to mind and imagination. Yet it was Bushnell who, although influenced significantly by German and English Romanticism, asserted in orthodox Pauline manner that unless Christ be formed in the human personality (Gal. 4:19) the incarnate word remains nothing but a cracked and paltry reflection of its human origin. That Bushnell was inspired by the romanticists' intuitive knowledge of God failed to nullify an epistemology rooted in the Puritan tradition. For him, natural supernaturalism and Christian regeneration never blurred into a merged oneness.

The groundwork of Christian Reformed thought earlier had been laid by John Calvin, whose system rests upon the absolute distinction between the glory of God and the sin-

fulness of man. Calvin did not scorn humanistic learning, but
he insisted that without saving grace the seeker after truth
ends only at the human point from which he started. In seeking God, he fails to rise above himself. Instead he measures
the divine by his own yardstick; he only imagines divinity out
of the fashioning of his presuppositions. To Calvin the imagination, like all natural capacities including reason, is energized by sin (self-righteousness) and leads to delusion. The
essential point is that Calvin's God is beyond self, beyond the
mythical gods and idols of the imagination, and beyond all
other imaginings. God's glory is free from the restraints by
which humans would make it comprehensible, and radically
separate ("de-humanized") from what a later Romantic era
glorified as the transcendental subjectivity of universal man.
Karl Barth and Reinhold Niebuhr made certain of that.

In American thought no one more clearly has drawn distinctions between natural and regenerate imagination than
Jonathan Edwards, whose exposition constitutes the subject
of the first chapter of the present book. Pauline in doctrine
and epistemology, Edwards believed that only as the heart is
redirected or converted (re-formed) toward God are human
works worthy of celebration, and then only as reflections of
the greater divine light. The *conditio sine qua non* was God's
sovereignty and glory. By contrast, the absolute truth for the
Romantic was the natural mind and all that passed in it. The
temptation to gloss over the contrast has led certain revision-
ists like Sacvan Bercovitch and Charles Feidelson, to name
but two legatees of Perry Miller, to claim a continuity between American Puritanism and subsequent Romanticism.
The claim clears the way to interpret Jonathan Edwards's
"sense of the heart" as a proto-Romantic experiential orientation, as if the experience Edwards recounted in *Personal Narrative* sounded a prelude to Thoreau's larger orchestration in
Walden. To assess the former experience through the eyes of
the latter, often with additional aesthetic interpolation, leads
to a deceptive softening of Puritan rigor and a diluting of the
integrity of Christian vision. My own argument presses for an
interpretation that finds discontinuity between a sense of the
heart and an intuitive knowledge.

Personifying this radical distinction are the saint and the artist, a conflict in theory as well as in dramatic personification so urgent as to have preoccupied the creative life of Nathaniel Hawthorne, the subject of chapter 2. Hawthorne confronted two opposing world views, two differing epistemologies, and two fundamental and conflicting interpretations of God, nature, and self. The ramifications of these colliding realities, one Calvinist and the other Romantic, penetrated and permeated his deepest consciousness which, like an immense spiderweb of the finest threads, caught the subtlest airborne particles of the issue. Jonathan Edwards and Nathaniel Hawthorne, each serving as either the theological or the artistic gloss for the other, envisioned with powerful attention where the two views led and what the consequences of commitment to one or the other were. For many reasons is Hawthorne's *The Scarlet Letter* an American classic, but surely one has to do with the opposing views personified in Dimmesdale and Hester, whose exaltation, anxiety, and sense of being obtain from within strikingly antithetical contexts.

I think it not preemptory in the next two chapters to pass over other major figures in favor of the relatively minor literary immigrants, Ole Rölvaag and John Muir. To have continued in the nineteenth-century mainstream would have been to consider the likes of Herman Melville, Mark Twain, Emily Dickinson, and Henry James, each of whom depicted in chiaroscuro the collisons and confusions stemming from an inherited dualism; it also would have been to study religious thinkers such as Bushnell, Ralph Waldo Emerson, Charles Hodge, Josiah Royce, and William James. But to consider representative immigrant writers highlights other persons, largely neglected, who brought to America strong ideas that did not fit into what Frederick Jackson Turner said was the country's evolving process of civilization associated with Westering. The problem with Turner's metaphor of process was that it failed to work experientially. It served the historian who, in taking his clue from Hegel and Emerson, saw history as projecting cosmic order. It served the poet, especially the Romantic elegist Walt Whitman, who, in gazing upon the grass of graves, rhapsodized, "O perpetual transfers and promotions." But it failed the Dakota farmer watching grasshoppers destroy his wheat or the mother hearing that her son had been killed at Shiloh. The metaphor of process neglected the exceptional in favor of the general and led to a historical perspective in which the concerns of individuals, including their motives, decisions, and anxieties, were submerged into the myths of garden and frontier.

Why Turner, Henry Nash Smith, and Leo Marx, despite their full research, chose to ignore the influx of immigrant millions attests obliquely to the fact that many immigrants resisted these Romantic myths. A corrective interpretation comes in Oscar Handlin's important study, *The Uprooted* (Boston: Little, Brown, 1951, 1973), in which he argued that immigrants felt estranged from America and constantly pressured to make themselves into something different from what they were. According to Handlin, their experience was more often a "cataclysmic plunge into the unknown" and a psychic crisis of devastating magnitude rather than a merging into the organic flow of a mythicized American history.

Both Rölvaag and Muir, sturdy immigrant writers that they were, embodied the very clash bespoken in an inherited Christian orthodoxy versus a new Romantic freedom and myth. Both writers brought to the American frontier an established religious perspective, one rooted in Norwegian Haugeanism and the other in Scottish Calvinism. For both writers, their religious inheritance clashed with the American myth of the frontier, including the symbolic advancements such as newness and fullness of being (rebirth) that supposedly accompanied the Western apotheosis. Rölvaag made clear that this clash constituted a true "frontier" experience and had to be reckoned with. The stakes in the conflict were not only cultural but religious. However, as seen in the troubled pair of Per Hansa and Beret in *Giants in the Earth,* the stakes had less to do with cultural assimilation than with salvation or damnation. Important also is the fact that Rölvaag's frontier grew out of conceptual dichotomies he had wrestled with from reading the works of Sören Kierkegaard, the Danish religious thinker who had raised the issue of either/ or to ultimate reference.

It needs to be noted that Rölvaag's frontier was not the same as Muir's, though to both writers the individual person was seen in experiential primacy. The difference between their two conceptions indicated a divided stream in Romanticism itself in which on the one hand, the self confronts nature and attempts to subdue and conquer it, and, on the other, the self seeks to merge with nature, to know its mysteries and discover personal identity as being part and parcel of the cosmic whole. Muir's frontier was this latter primitivism, the material of myth and mythical consciousness. What can be called a rediscovered primitivism was later to infuse the poetry of such Western writers as Robinson Jeffers and Theodore Roethke. But Muir, like Rölvaag, typified the immigrant caught between one consciousness rooted in time and place, and another that expanded into the infinities. Though Muir inclined powerfully toward Romanticism, including mountain grandeur and all of nature's ministrations, his incumbent Calvinism was not to be effaced or reconciled. A faint but deep fissure etched through his inner world.

For every writer, whatever his heritage, the age-old problem has been what to do with the self: whether to affirm it mightily, to lose it in mystical reality, to accept its finitude and corruptibility, to mask it behind aesthetic form, and so on. Increasingly evident in recent times is the danger of a privileged and autonomous self, the origin and measure of all reality. In this Romantic consummation is to be seen the self's own destruction—or its ennui, impotence, and negation—unless the self can be persuaded or deluded to justify its raison d'être with works wrought by the imagination. In a world that Robert Frost feared was devoid of ultimate meaning, including a frontier stretching away to the edge of doom, he faced the choice between the claims of art and those of religion, between a Romanticism that still postulated an independent self despite a teleological West drained of value and, by contrast, a religious orthodoxy that affirmed a radically different ontology. That he chose the protective stratagems of self to keep at bay all that was not self may be seen as the choice art requires of all true disciples, and the consequences may eventuate in the same terrible price that art exacts.

In the present study, the chapter that explores these matters centers on Frost, a Californian by birth who returned to his New England roots to find them withered except for what fructifying energy he supplied, a Romanticism of desperation. Upon this thread he wagered his conceptual integrity, and with its collapse he faced the dark terror.

The final chapter posits a world of ultimate wagers where Romanticism and Christian consciousness vie, and where every artist and saint, critic and religious thinker, is obliged to acknowledge selfhood and face the encroachments that this responsibility quickens. If one's labyrinth of solitude contains several Ariadne threads—for example, aestheticism, ethical humanism, mythical consciousness, Christian hope—the decision to follow a single thread becomes a matter of ultimate concern, for each thread has its own direction, not all threads lead to liberation, and some take the solitary wanderer back into even deeper and more dreadful vacancies.

I need to acknowledge my indebtedness to those persons from whom I drew assistance and support while writing this book. I especially want to mention the staff of the Norwegian-American Historical Association at St. Olaf College, Northfield, Minnesota. I honed certain ideas against the critical intelligence of colleagues, and I would be remiss in failing to mention two: Professors Malcolm Brown and Kenneth Requa. For permission to reprint material in which parts of this book first appeared, I thank the editors of *Andover Newton Quarterly, Scandinavian Studies, Western American Literature,* and *Texas Quarterly.* Finally, I am grateful for the abiding interest that my daughter and two sons have shown in my work, and the special support given me by my wife, to whom this book is dedicated.

Radical Discontinuities

1
Typology, Imagination, and Jonathan Edwards

I

It was not the "self" that William Bradford's pilgrims celebrated when they stepped ashore on the windswept coast of Cape Cod. Nor, as they faced the "hideous and desolate wilderness," did they envision their security as resting on democratic hopes. What they praised was "the God of Heaven who had brought them over the vast and furious ocean," and what they established was a community based upon not only a mutual compact but also a covenant with God.[1] They were not so innocent as to entrust their precarious New England foothold to human resources alone, whether those of a single leader or a collective rule. Their errand had been commissioned by an authority whose power transcended their own.

Even so, the Bradford group lacked the truly radical vision that informed the more organized Puritans aboard the *Arabella* ten years later. This vision was that of a Boston modeled on Christian love, a society of Christian saints knit each to each by love, the one body bonded to God through membership in "the body of Christ." To love one's brother and obey God's commandments was a more radical commitment than to rebel against a tyrannical king or archbishop. Nevertheless, Boston was to be a theocracy where sainthood would be visible and governable. Here was to be a new Israel

19

where "temporals" and "spirituals" would be reconciled through a covenant between Boston and God. As it proved, John Winthrop's "A Model of Christian Charity" was indeed a more radical document in its substance and implications than the one written 146 years later declaring national independence.

Neither disobedience nor uncharitableness would destroy the covenant, for in reality it was a covenant sealed by God through Christ. Within the bond, a person was to be punished for sin and blessed for righteousness, but the question was never one of autonomy outside the bond. What vitalized the covenant was the quality of love *(caritas)*. Love, said Winthrop, is "absolutely necessary"; it is "a real thing[,] *not imaginary.*"[2] The city as a promised, a commanded, and finally a revealed thing was the locus where God's holiness and love would have its terrestrial counterpart among New England's saints. Winthrop did more than imagine or assess this vision. To do either requires an independent will and a certain detachment. He proclaimed it in language that sprang from firsthand faith; his sacramental vision could not have existed apart from this foundation. His language entered into a different realm where poetic metaphor did not hold and symbolic thinking did not rule. For Winthrop and his congregation of visible saints, the city was not an imaginative trope or figure created by a fertile imagination but a type revealed through faith.

What is frequently overlooked in understanding the Puritan experience is this typological basis—that is, the way in which the Puritans interpreted their venture as one that had been prefigured by events in the Old Testament. One typological tradition that they inherited was the conservative Antiochean way of reading scripture, restricting typology to Old Testament "types" and their New Testament "antitypes,"a relationship by which the New Testament Christ, for example, was interpreted as fulfilling the meaning of the Old Testament Adam. The only extension that conservative exegetes allowed was to carry the meaning of antitypes into biblical history. A more far-reaching tradition, inspired by

Alexandrian exegetes such as Philo, Clement, and Origen, extended Old Testament types/New Testament antitypes into the spiritual experience of the believer as well as into his communal present. New England Puritans inherited both these traditions, which had influenced a thousand years of exegetical study, but found special relevance in the extension that made their New England experience the historical fulfillment of the Israelites' journey into Canaan. Many Puritan typologists such as Edward Johnson, John Davenport, Samuel Danforth, and Samuel Mather explained this extension as having been decreed by God, whose prerogative it was to make "types." In the same year that Winthrop identified Boston to be the city God had placed upon a hill for all the world to see, John Cotton made explicit the typological significance of the new kingdom by calling it the "land of Canaan," the promised land. Again, the language used is not merely figurative to elicit imagination; it is typological and presupposes for its understanding the faith of the interpreter living "in Christ." We must, Cotton exhorted, discern how God appoints His people to the promised land by discerning "themselves to be in Christ . . . and by finding his holy presence with them."[3] For his treatise, "God's Promise to His Plantation" (1630), Cotton used the text from 2 Sam. 7:10: "Moveover I will appoint a place for my people Israel, and I will plant them, that they may dwell in a place of their own, and move no more."

The masterpiece of typological interpretation was Cotton Mather's *Magnalia Christi Americana* (1702), the ecclesiastical history of New England purporting to show "Christ's Great Deeds in America." Even Vernon Louis Parrington, whose sympathies could hardly be said to extend to Mather ("What a crooked and diseased mind lay back of those eyes," he wrote), recognized the *Magnalia* as "the *magnum opus* of Massachusetts theocracy."[4] Indeed, nothing in American literature compares with this book. Almost like some ancient epic poet, Mather announces his great theme in the opening sentence: "I write of the wonders of the Christian religion, flying from the deprivations of Europe, to the American

strand." What needs emphasizing, however, is that Mather
did not think himself a poet, inspired by pagan muses, but a
regenerate Christian living in Christ. Through spiritual dis-
cernment Mather celebrates New England's fulfillment of
biblical "types." In the *Magnalia* America signifies the victory of the Blessed Remnant ("this little Israel") over Satan's
world. His account takes his "actors" out of Europe, across
the Atlantic, and into the American wilderness where they
plant a colony (books I, II, and III); establish a Christian
theocracy (books IV and V); and, in a series of "remarkable
providences" eventuating in triumphs over Satan (books VI
and VII), prepare for the return of Christ to a "renovated
world." Mather's work was more than a jeremiad to warn the
city on the hill to mend its backsliding ways, and more than a
poetical epic informed by myth. The *Magnalia* was a work of
history written from within the circle of faith and in defiance
of what he calls "an evil generation." More importantly, it
was salvation-history, telling how the Remnant as "type,"
representing the chosen Hebrews, prefigured the Puritan
"antitype," and how the errand into the American wilderness
was part of church history and part of God's preordained
scheme of redemption.

At issue is the intentional force antecedent to the generic
form. According to Sacvan Bercovitch, a "gargantuan" imagination impelled Mather, the typologist, to interpret John
Cotton as the antitype of Moses, John Norton as that of
Joshua, Winthrop as that of Nehemiah, and Boston as the
conclusive antitype of Jerusalem. Instead of Mather's debt to
Origen, who extended Old Testament types and New Testament antitypes to include the church—and to Augustine who,
in searching for significance in human events, subsumed history *(Historie)* into salvation-history *(Heilsgeschichte)*—
Bercovitch cites Mather's imagination as the informing impulse. Ultimately, instead of Christian faith in providential
history, it was imagination, according to Bercovitch, that was
the power behind Mather's grand conception, making Mather
in the end an artist, a symbolist, and a mythmaker.[5]

As between faith and imagination as ways of knowing, an

interpretation of Puritanism that rests its case upon the shaping power of the Puritan imagination falls short of explaining the groundwork of typological exegesis. The countless ways early Americans interpreted providential history did not mean they sacrificed biblical literalism but rather that they apprehended (spiritually discerned) a correspondence existing between literal scripture and its spiritual meaning. This correspondence also embraced secular and redemptive history. Although the Reformers earlier had adopted this view in their reaction to the traditional fourfold exegetical method of the medievalists (literal, moral, allegorical, anagogical), it remained for the American Puritans to explain how typology applied to their covenanted community and their individual practice. In all this, the boldest exegete was Jonathan Edwards, whose typological reading of scripture extended to history, nature, and creation itself. But the underlying issue remains epistemological, namely, the nature of the perceiver whose perceptions inform his knowing. Without making the radical distinction between the faith of a twice-born Puritan and the imagination of a once-born Romantic, there is nothing particularly momentous in Bercovitch's claim that Mather's soteriological vision was inverted into Emerson's New World history; that the Puritan, who once stood before a sovereign God, became instead the new American Romantic who subsumed the concept of *sola fide* into the doctrine of faith-in-self-alone; and, finally, that this new American self was a "deific creation *ex imaginatione* in which *caritas* depended upon autonomy, and plenitude was narcissism extended to infinity." For, as Bercovitch's argument emphasizes, imagination is the key to it all, the American self is a grand artistic creation of its own, and it always has been. The great American myth, of which Mather's *Magnalia* partakes, is in reality "a testament to the visionary and symbolic power of the American Puritan imagination."[6]

In resting his case on imagination Bercovitch misses the deeper fiduciary mystery that informed the Puritan view of history's true design. An interesting corollary appears in Charles Feidelson's argument that imagination was exactly what the Puritans lacked. Although the two views appear to oppose each other, they ironically unite in missing the radical and experiential faith that served as the groundwork of what can be called Puritan perception. Feidelson points to the Puritans' "science of typology" as evidence of their "characteristic narrowness" of thought. Seeing in the Puritan system of typological correspondence little more than rational literalism, which supposedly mirrored the zealous way they sought intellectual understanding of God's great mechanism, Feidelson argues that the Puritans "were doomed to pay for their mistake." They paid for their fear of imagination and their fear of symbolic thinking with a diminished art. Moreover, as an obiter dictum, what Feidelson calls "the crudity or conventionality of a great part of American literature from 1620 through the third quarter of the nineteenth century" may be attributed, he thinks, "to inherited mental habits which proscribed a functional artistic form."[7]

More subtle than Parrington's prejudice is the pervasive notion that the Puritans must in some way be saved from themselves, either through their intellect, imagination, or moral sternness. As if in grateful resolution, readers harken to the fact that the Puritans did, after all, establish Harvard; produce vast quantities of theological and devotional treatises, verse, philosophy, biography, history, and scientific writings (Cotton Mather's bibliography would have had to include 450 publications); and nurture a moral strength that seemed as enduring as their rockbound coast. That they also held to a stony Calvinism with its warning against delusions of self-grandeur and the hell of autonomy makes some readers feel obliged to do their rescue work. A common strategy, for example, is to show that in actuality the distance between Edwards and Emerson is not so disjunctive after all. In Perry Miller's well-known essay, the two thinkers nearly join souls in the mystical presence of nature. Admittedly, says Miller, Edwards would have denounced "to the nethermost circle of Hell" the suggestion that his thought could be called mysticism or pantheism, but such, argues Miller, is nevertheless implicit "in the texture, if not the logic" of it. All that supposedly prevented Edwards from affirming the Emersonian Over-Soul was a vexing orthodox theology—"supposedly derived from the Word of God, which taught that God and nature are not one, that man is corrupt and his self-reliance is reliance on evil." Miller's furtive suggestion is: "But take away the theology, remove this overlying stone of dogma from the wellspring of Puritan conviction, and both nature and man become divine."[8] Feidelson's Orwellian excision of theology is equally deft: "Theology aside, Edwards anticipated the symbolic consciousness of Emerson," by which Feidelson means that Edwards shared Emerson's conviction that intuition surpasses logic.[9] We are left with the fact, however, that, unlike Emerson, Edwards did not put aside his theology with its baleful warnings against natural intuition. In short, the pervasive argument among literary readers presupposes a blight upon the Puritan mind—a stony dogma to be rolled away, a letter to be discarded, so that the natural energies including those of creativity can have their effulgent way. Perhaps less subtle but nonetheless consistent with this attitude is Parrington's complaint that the "tragedy" of Edwards's intellectual life was that "the theologian triumphed over the philosopher."[10] For literary critics the complaint is the triumph of the theologian over the artist. Either way, the modern reader can neutralize the tragedy by surgically removing the unwanted theology and thus transforming Edwards, say, into a "precursor" of nineteenth-century transcendentalists, notably the liberating Emerson.[11]

If it is thought the Puritans paid the price of a diminished art for being wary of an unbridled self, it may also be thought the Romantics paid a higher price for their vaunted divinity and their triumphant art. Nothing is without its cost, including art and religious martyrdom. The Puritans suspected art, however, to exact a greater cost. That they feared symbolic thinking in interpreting types was not because of psychological timidity or deficiency of soul but rather a religious conviction that natural imagination wrought idols. A poetic symbol might be no less an idol than a golden calf. The Puritans had no intention to abolish figurative language because such lan-

guage, taken from nature, was legitimate for purposes of
rhetorical effect. The danger, they believed, was when symbol usurped type—when imagination usurped revelation as
the means of spiritual truth. What they feared was not the
symbol or metaphor per se but the imagination from which
the figures sprang; moreover, they feared imagination because they believed it perverted the act of perception. "Men
must not indulge their own Fancies . . . except we have some
Scripture ground for it," Samuel Mather admonished; "it is
not safe to make any thing a Type meerly upon our own
fancies and imaginations; it is Gods Perogative [sic] to make
Types."[12] Mather's warning is in mistaking what might be
called the ontology of imagination for that of faith, wherein
the created symbol in the one challenges the spiritual reality
inherent in the other. To substitute imagination for faith was
the surest way to damnation, and the Puritans feared this to
be the price of art.

The audacious faith of Edwards affirmed God's revelation
not only in historical events and individual acts but in nature
itself. To him the sun, for example, was to be seen not merely
as an object imaginatively transformed for use as a decorative
image to serve the artist's rhetorical purpose (though such a
use he considered legitimate), and decidedly not as a symbolic
extension of the artist's mind. Edwards saw the sun as a
type—as a sign of God's creative spirit, a revelation of his
ontological truth. The typological meaning of light was intended to be that of spiritual light. Instead of a poetic image,
the sun was seen as a divine image shadowing forth, as it
were, God's excellency and glory.

In America, Edwards was the archspokesman for the Puritan orthodox belief that such light was seen only by one who
received through grace the gift of true sight. To natural man
no such gift has been given. But to the regenerate, who lives
in Christ, a new sense of things, a new way of perceiving, is
made available. In his *Personal Narrative* Edwards described
this alteration: "After this my sense of divine things gradually
increased, and became more and more lively. . . . The appearance of every thing was altered; there seemed to be, as it were,

a calm, sweet cast, or appearance of divine glory, in almost every thing."[13] Whether in thunder and lightning or in sunshine and grass, Edwards perceived the "great and glorious God." If this be "narrowness" of thought, as Feidelson intimates, Edwards would wish that all persons be granted such vision. The Puritans believed their visionary span exceeded anything that originated from the imagination sui generis.

In typological language, therefore, the sun was not a poetic image or metaphor but a divine image, not a trope but a type. The trope stems from a "lively notion of an outward thing," useful in rhetoric, but the type or divine image is "that of which spiritual reality consists in itself."[14]

We begin to sense the danger in considering Edwards as the precursor of Emerson. The claim can be made definitive only by disregarding the fact that, whereas Edwards grounded his typological reading of nature in a scriptural Logos, Emerson based his interpretation on a Platonic idealism that swallowed time and place into eternal myth. Neither this distinction nor yet another can be expunged, namely, the difference between so-called natural and regenerate perception. Edwards's Calvinism would have yielded no ground to the bruited insistence from transcendentalists that *everyone* was endowed essentially with spiritual perception. For Edwards a radical discontinuity marked the natural and the regenerate creature, and only by the latter, who, in Christ, has received a wholly new capacity to see, is the spiritual image understood. Emerson, on the contrary, liberated everyone from a sinful world. He rejected the distinction between natural and regenerate, and in equating natural with divine he proclaimed all creatures to be one with God in nature. In "Circles" Emerson preached a life of new and ever-expanding circles, without end. Acknowledging no limitation, no walls of mortality, no state of fallenness or sin, every man "fills the sky" and thus stands ready to declare, "I am God in nature." In his "Divinity School Address" Emerson sought to reassure every person that the old Puritan creed, which "is passing away," must certainly not interfere with one's self-declared infinitude.

Before taking up Edwards's specific ideas about imagina-

tion and its perilous ways, we need to pay still closer attention to the crucial issue that begins to emerge at this point of
typological interpretation. It concerns a way of knowing and
seeing, a perspective by which reality as divine creation is
affirmed. Specifically, the issue has to do with the gift of faith
and the sight issuing from a regenerate consciousness. Whatever else regeneration implies, a fundamental principle of it
establishes a new vision radically different from that of natural understanding and sight. According to classical Protestant
theology, the ultimate object is not a set of doctrinal proposi-
tions to which a person gives assent, nor is it a world created
and shaped by natural imagination; it is a personal reality of
God through Christ, a relationship founded in one's response
to the divine grace revealed in God's Word, incarnated in the
Son, and addressed to human beings by the Holy Spirit
through the word and sacraments of the gospel. Outside this
relationship the natural (fallen) man stands alone or, at best,
in relationship with nature and its divinities, but he remains
blind to the Christian truth of his fallen condition and the
means of regeneration. The American Romantics later would
come to celebrate this separateness as freedom and preach
reunion with nature's gods as true regeneration.

The all-important consideration in distinguishing between
what Winthrop had earlier called "this real thing" and what
the Romantics hailed as an imagined thing was the nature of
the perceiver. The exegete, for example, who perceived spiritual meaning supposedly possessed a special capacity separating him from others and making him capable of comprehend-
ing the "soul" of the text and, by extension, the spiritual
meaning of history. To be in the "body of Christ" was to
have been crucified and resurrected with Christ, to have experienced the Incarnation by living in and with Christ (Col.
2:9–13). To have the indwelling spirit of God through Christ
made the distinction unequivocal. According to Paul, "we,"
the spiritually elect, have received "the spirit which is of God;
that we might know the things that are freely given to us of
God"; whereas "the natural man receiveth not the things of
the Spirit of God: for they are foolishness unto him: neither

can he know them, because they are spiritually discerned" (1 Cor. 2:12, 14). According to the Apostle Matthew, Jesus had made the same distinction in saying to his disciples that by the same gift of grace "it is given unto you to know the mysteries of the kingdom of heaven, but to them [the unregenerate] it is not given" (Matt. 13:11).

Regenerate perception enabled one to see what he could not see before, namely, the spiritual meanings in scripture, history, nature, and, as Edwards believed, in all creation. The special meanings visible only to regenerate eyes are described by Edwards in rhapsodic utterance:

> In the creature's knowing, esteeming, loving, rejoicing in and praising God, the glory of God is both *exhibited* and *acknowledged;* his fulness is *received* and *returned.* Here is both *emanation* and *remanation.* The refulgence shines upon and into the creature, and is reflected back to the luminary. The beams of glory come from God, and are something of God, and are refunded back again to their original. So that the whole is *of* God, and *in* God, and *to* God, and he is the beginning, and the middle, and the end.[15]

The passage is understandable according to its epistemological presuppositions. What we know depends upon how we know. According to Edwards, what we know about Christian truth and specifically about the emanation of God's glory depends upon the revelation of divine spirit in terms of light. Only after God initiates this light of grace are his highest attributes perceived, but perceived after the event of regeneration, the saving man-God event through Christ. This event, Edwards said, takes place in the heart, in the ravished and transformed heart, in the core of human beingness, including man's reason and his consenting will. Thus the redeemed heart is both the *what* and the *how* of Christian knowledge. All subsequent perception stems from this new foundation of being. Accordingly, what we know depends upon how we know, which in turn, depends upon what we are. This identity is illumined by the light that natural man neither comprehends nor extinguishes.

Knowledge based upon natural reason—important as such knowledge was to Puritan theology, cosmology, historiography, and rhetoric—was never intended to serve as ultimate truth. Even in its limitations, however, natural reason did not pose the dangers that were thought to accompany visions generated by natural imagination. The Puritans meditated hard and long on Jeremiah's denunciation of the Israelites who heeded "the imagination of their evil heart" (Jer. 3:17), and took even more seriously Paul's excoriations of natural men who, boasting of their knowledge of God, "became vain in their imaginations" (Rom. 1:21) and foolish in their darkened hearts. Echoing the earlier patriarchs, he warned against any imaginative analogy linking God with "gold, or silver, or stone, graven by art and man's device," or with, in the words of the Revised Standard version, "a representation by the art and imagination of man" (Acts 17:29). Paul did not scorn the use of reason and imagination per se, or the use of symbol as an aid to worship. But he emphatically argued that the knowledge of God cannot be reached through these means and, like Jeremiah, warned against the symbol that becomes a barrier or a substitute for a genuine encounter with God. He insisted, as did the Puritans, that the knowledge of God is reached through the awakened soul and consciousness. Only the power of the divine spirit opens blind eyes. True spiritual awareness was the power to see and the capacity to respond. The Puritans' suspicion of art lay in their impulse to reject whatever substituted for the God-man relationship or stood in the way of mediation. The barrier to religious knowledge was not thought to be doubt but sinful pride, broken only when God reduced man and all his works of hand and imagination to creatureliness under judgment. To suppose divine power irrelevant and natural capacities adequate to human spiritual needs was the very mark of sin.

II

In the writings of Jonathan Edwards the question of natural and regenerate imagination finds its most important Puri-

tan treatment. The issue stems from the radical Pauline dualism between nature and spirit, and branches out into the
epistemological differences between imagination and faith as
sources of knowledge, and between artist and saint as know-
ers. Some critics have interpreted Edwards as (merely) an
artist, a conclusion resolving the dualism once and for all.
Concerning the specific artistry of Edwards's famous "Sinners in the Hands of an Angry God," Edwin H. Cady's
analysis of imagery has become something of a critical
model.[16] Recent studies indicate the subject to be ever more
in vogue. The time is not far off, one critic writes, when
Edwards's works will be read "as literary through and
through"— meaning that even though the twentieth-century
reader thinks Edwards's ideas are "dead, old-fashioned,
quaint," such a reader still can have access to Edwards's artistry.[17] Notwithstanding the fact that many other readers
consider Edwards's ideas as anything but dead—as, in fact,
urgent and relevant—the one-sided interpretation of Edwards
as an artist fails to do justice to him as a Christian thinker and
to the whole subject of art and the imagination from his
Christian point of view. To come to grips with this subject
may correct what has become a distorted emphasis. For it is
Edwards's concept of the imagination and its theological basis
that must first be understood before one can even tentatively
call Edwards an imaginative artist, a designation he himself
never claimed.

Edwards's concept of imagination squarely rests upon the
eighteenth-century distinction between speculative knowledge (thought) and sensible knowledge (sensation and feeling). Imagination belongs to the latter. Knowledge derived
from speculation alone never satisfactorily answered Edwards's great religious questions about sin, faith, grace, and
holiness. Cognition never opened the deeper levels of consciousness where he did his theological work. An alternative
for Edwards was sensible knowledge: knowledge that springs
from feelings and engages a greater portion of human personality. This knowledge creates within the mind a sense of
things, an intuited conviction, a sight that transforms abstract

truth into "actual ideas" inseparable from feeling.[18] According to Edwards, sense perception enhanced by imagination
quickens the mind to natural beauty, to sounds and sights, to
appetites, even to something he regarded as natural good and
evil. Such knowledge, surpassing "mere notion," may even
bring to natural man a sense of "God's greatness, power and
awful majesty," as well as a sense of human finitude and
guilt.[19]

   This twofold division between thought and feeling—hardly
as arbitrary as I have suggested here, yet fundamental in Edwards's epistemology—breaks into yet another division: nature and spirit.[20] Thought is both natural and spiritual: feelings, likewise, are those that all natural men experience and
those that only the regenerate know. Going either the way of
thought or of feeling, one finally arrives at this other distinction which separates the thoughts and feelings of natural man
from those of the regenerate man. This distinction is ordained
by God through Christ, and it is the basis of Christian
knowledge. On this matter Edwards stood firm. Regardless
of how far one goes with speculative knowledge, or how
much farther with so-called sensible knowledge, for Edwards
the way stops at that point where the Pauline distinction
between nature and spirit becomes real.

   That imagination belongs to sensible rather than speculative knowledge serves to distinguish imagination from reason
and the ways of notional thought. In his early essay "Of the
Prejudice of Imagination," inserted into *Notes on "The
Mind,"* Edwards denounced those persons who supposedly
had "conquered" imagination. He was emboldened to suggest
that the reason certain unnamed thinkers still preferred
Ptolemy was that they could not tolerate what their imagination conceived as a vaster universe. Edwards here is referring
to natural imagination or to what Leon Howard calls the
"philosophical or unregenerate imagination," the endowment
of natural man. The point has to do not so much with the
rationalists' being unable to yield to the revelations of the
imagination but to their clinging to what the natural imagination, based in and restricted to sense, reports to them of the

universe. Of more concern to Edwards was the "regenerate imagination" (again Professor Howard's term) that owes its quality to the event of conversion.[21] Both kinds of imagination extend from the dichotomy between the natural and the spiritual.

Although the importance Edwards gave to the concept of imagination may not readily appear in his total writings, it is important to note that he lived at a time when the term "imagination" was in crucial transition. The old scholastic meaning still persisted, in Edwards and in others, while at the same time the new Romantic meaning was growing, with the latter having the present-day connotation of creativity. Stages describing this transition show that, in the first place, Christian theologians earlier had asserted that the "book of nature" demonstrates divine purpose in the universe, to be read in the light of revelation; whereas by Edwards's day this emphasis was being reversed, and revelation was to be read by the light of nature, including natural reason and understanding. Thinkers such as the third earl of Shaftesbury (Anthony Ashley Cooper), Henry More, and other Cambridge Platonists grew ever closer to substituting communion with nature for communion in the sacrament. Secondly, the older epistemology posited that the natural mind cannot form a real image of God, that the infinite is the nonimaginable opposite of the finite, and that no natural man can derive any conception of the Supreme Being. What John Locke came to argue, on the other hand, was that the whole idea of God arises from sensory experiences, thus eliminating the necessity of revelation. We have "no other idea of him, but a complex one of existence, knowledge, power, happiness, etc., infinite and eternal . . . originally got from sensation and reflection."[22] Thirdly, by the eighteenth century, ideas of the divine took on a visual quality; God's immensity was seen as commensurable with space and his glory with nature's sublimity. Providence was synonymous with natural law. As for imagination, Locke thought of it as a natural instrument of perception. Thomas Hobbes went further to suggest that imagination discovers new harmonies within dissimilitudes. With Joseph Addison's papers on "Pleasures of the Imagination" (1712) reason was all but eliminated from imaginative perception, and imagination extended sensuous (sensible) experience to produce a spiritual effect. Thus for Addison, whom Jonathan Edwards read, imagination "served as a means of reconciling man with his spiritual needs and his desire to belong to a living universe of purpose and value."[23] Imagination was the gracious means of receiving the impressions of nature, itself the unfoldment of divinity, and also of creating illusion that served as the poet's revelation to man. With the theoretical foundations well laid by other eighteenth-century thinkers like Francis Hutchinson, Mark Akenside, John Baillie, and Alexander Gerard, the Romantic soul could soar on the wings of poesy, could inhabit the supernatural world, indeed could create and reveal it.

In his *Distinguishing Marks of a Work of the Spirit of God* (1741) Edwards cautiously acknowledged human nature to be such that "we can't think of things invisible, without a degree of imagination." The more engaged the mind and intense the affections (Edwards's stellar objectives), "still the more lively and strong will the imaginary ideas ordinarily be."[24] To experience the "imaginary idea" as the "actual idea" (Locke), like fear or joy, is to know the idea as event. Edwards's concern here is with the imagination per se which bridges speculative and sensible knowledge, unifies the poles of reason and sensation, and thereby embraces the totality of natural existence. Functioning in this way the imagination mediates between intellect and sense.

Yet there is an all-important caveat that kept Edwards from going the way of Locke and the later theorists, even though he read Locke with avidity. Edwards remained steadfastly orthodox in his theology: natural man is sinful; moreover, anything that partakes in the condition of nature partakes as well in its condition of fallenness. Regardless of the power of imagination to receive the impressions of nature, to create its own world of aesthetic beauty, or to mediate between thought and feeling, Edwards never considered imagination a way to spiritual truth. Indeed, of man's natural capacities the imagination was the most susceptible to the devil's wiles. In the *Treatise Concerning Religious Affections* (1746) Edwards quoted with due seriousness the English Puritan Anthony Burgess: "The imagination is that room of the soul, wherein the devil doth often appear."[25] The reference is to natural imagination which, as such, is destitute of divine grace—the imagination from which, according to Burgess, "horrible" and "diabolical" delusions arise. Edwards did not need to go beyond his own Connecticut Valley for verification. After all, it was the horrendous imaginings of the Enthusiasts that he excluded from the legitimate and distinguishing marks of Christian experience. Strangely powerful though such imaginings were, he knew their danger if they were mistaken for divine revelation. Edwards never mitigated the truth of this fact. Although his own artistry rose to compelling intensity, awakening the imagination of those persons still decidedly numbered among the unregenerate; although his sermons crackled with the behest, "Imagine . . . Imagine . . .";[26] although his bursts of imagery left the audience no choice but to comply, his use of imagination having sufficed to bring to life both terror and tranquility; yet Edwards's concept of the imagination never pointed to it as producing spiritual effect. Persons guilty of such delusion failed to understand that in spite of the expansiveness that natural imagination commanded, the vision that was forthcoming was by definition limited and corrupt.

What troubled Edwards during the Great Awakening was not only the legalistic hypocrisy he saw among the Arminians but also the evangelistic hypocrisy among persons who were carried away by impulse and imagined revelations.[27] Thus he deemed it necessary to warn against imagination when he saw it counterfeiting true spiritual light. Distinguishing between what he considered the true and the false in religious matters, Edwards warned in *Some Thoughts Concerning the Present Revival* (1743) that natural imagination is never more than a "common gift" that all men possess.[28] Natural imaginings must not be mistaken for those inspired by divine agency. When Enthusiasts heard "voices" and beheld "visions," claimed that such revelations came from God, and then based their religious affections upon these experiences, Edwards knew the issue demanded stern clarification.

> Thus [he wrote in *Religious Affections*] when the Spirit of God gives a natural man visions, as he did Balaam, he only impresses a natural principle, viz. the sense of seeing, immediately exciting ideas of that sense; but he gives no new sense; neither is there anything supernatural, spiritual or divine in it. So if the Spirit of God impresses on a man's imagination, either in a dream, or when he is awake, any outward ideas of any of the senses, either voices, or shapes and colors, 'tis only exciting ideas of the same kind that he has by natural principles and senses.[29]

A person may have thousands of such "visions." His imagination may create varieties of religious experience that include the most sublime aesthetic moments. Yet to regard such experience as evidence of religious affection when the heart is devoid of grace is to be guilty of evangelistic pretense. Or to attribute transcendent perception to imagination alone, even for the saint, is Romantic fallacy. What Edwards held as necessary in order to perceive the invisible and spiritual is divine grace prior to and independent of imagination. Vivid and holy imaginings may then follow. This is not to say that the regenerate imagination would suddenly be free from the senses for its store of images but rather than its images would be validated as they arise from new spiritual knowledge and affections.

It was never Edwards's purpose to denigrate imagination and the aesthetic vision. On the contrary he often conceived of theological issues in aesthetic terms, beauty being an ontological model. The point, however, is that unaided natural imagination is never adequate to this conception of beauty. This is the real substance of Edwards's admonishment. Imagination untouched by grace yields no spiritual discoveries, it gives no new sense. It may enable natural man to have tentative conceptions about spiritual affections, but of the nucleus or kernel he has no more conception than one born blind has of colors. Adamant about these ultimate distinctions, Edwards averred that in matters pertaining to religious truth the spiritually destitute imagination leaves a person no better than "totally blind, deaf and senseless, yea dead."[30]

Danger arises when one thinks otherwise, obscuring the distinction between "lively imaginations arising from strong [religious] affections, and strong affections arising from lively imaginations."[31] The first is the way of blessedness and vision; the second, the way of pride and delusion. In the end Edwards's warning is profoundly simple: natural imagination embraces nothing unless the soul through faith first embraces God. Only then is the imagination sanctified; and for this, the redeemed heart is the *conditio sine qua non*.

The term "embrace" is Edwards's metaphor. Its meaning is radically different from what certain of his contemporaries as well as nineteenth-century Romantics suggested when they heralded the imagination as that which unifies all natural time and space, and then issues forth in art as a human apocalypse. As H. Richard Niebuhr reminds us, this kind of imagination is characterized by egotism: all the world is centered in the self.[32] In waging, as it were, a kind of counter-Copernican revolution, natural imagination thus establishes the universe as egocentric and all truth as solipsism. In contrast, the sanctified or regenerate imagination presupposes a consenting soul. In this connection Edwards used the word "embrace." By it he meant the act of one's believing, the soul's "entirely embracing . . . entirely adhering and acquiescing" in Christian revelation."[33] Only as the soul embraces or consents to the perfect excellency of God as revealed in Christ will the imagination discover "the beauty of the Godhead, and the divinity of Divinity . . . the good of the infinite Fountain of Good."[34] A person imagines nothing who does not through grace imagine this. Underlying the equation is Edwards's dictum: man first believes that he might then truly imagine. Whereas natural imagination makes man the center, regenerate imagination embraces all things and thus enables him to hope all things and to endure all things. In other words, when in man, the center cannot hold; when in God, it orders all things and through Christ unfolds them to our new sight.

Speculation about new sight that comes through grace raises important questions about the nature of religious imagination. To what extent can such imagination surpass the limitations of speculative reason and natural imagination? Furthermore, to what extent is it necessary to deny empirical knowledge to make room for religious faith? In what way does faith enable one to see more clearly even though the glass of vision is never perfect? Does religious imagination answer questions about the meaning of man, his destiny, his highest goal, more satisfactorily than philosophic thought? What is to prevent any individual from claiming such powers of sight and then acting capriciously upon them?

In answering such problems Edwards returned again and again to special grace as differentiated from common grace that merely assists the faculties in doing more fully what they already do by nature. Special grace, Edwards argued, "causes the faculties to do that which they do not by nature and of which there is nothing of the like kind in the soul by nature."[35] The gift of special grace is the sanctified imagination. Not only does the regenerate receive a new foundation and inclination of will but, according to Edwards, he possesses a new imaginative power by which to apprehend what before was invisible. Edwards called these apprehensions "illuminations," the foremost being those of glory. Essential in Edwards's thought is the fact that God is the Creator of the new capacity to see. God's own glory is seen when conversion first brings one into this glory. Imagination embraces it because the believer stands within its circle.

Although Edwards's basis for religious imagination is singularly theological, one should not suppose that theology was only theoretical and logical to Edwards. When citing special grace as the underlying answer to questions about imagination, he did not mean that these questions suddenly lost their mystery. Edwards never intended theology to simplify matters, nor did he think theology simple. Theology carried the same risks as did life because Edwards knit both together according to decisions of belief that defied logical verification. That through grace religious imagination makes possible spiritual illuminations beyond normal experience was for Edwards a faith that demanded the commitment of his total self. It was this totality that was at stake in the decisions of belief. A theological answer was a religious one, together affirming the mystery as well as the spiritual sense that perceives it.

On this subject Richard Kroner suggests that imagination "can perform its religious function only when man from whom imagination springs is included in the divine mystery, or, more precisely, when it is this mystery itself that works in man."[36] This mysterious force customarily termed inspiration implies a power at work within man but greater than his own creative energy. It engenders religious imagination which, as Kroner says, bridges the gap between man and the divine mystery. The notion here is that religious imagination, no less mysterious than its content or product, is inspiration from the side of man and divine revelation from the side of God. Through imagination sanctified by God's spirit the saint sees everything as related to divine mystery. As Kroner points out, the world no longer exists merely for man's practical use, theoretical speculation, or aesthetic intuition. The saint sees the world stamped as part of divine creation and subject to God's intervening wrath and love. He sees everything in the world as consisting of images or shadows of divine things. The world is not only symbolical but sacramental in the sense that the regenerate eye beholds it as existing within the unity of divine meaning. It is this sacramental dimension that Edwards believed is only visible to the sanctified imagination, for there is no sacramental object apart from the special heartfelt sense that grasps it.

When Edwards referred to the sanctified sense, he meant the new spiritual sense that God graciously gives, enabling man to perceive the miraculous element in all phenomena.[37] Seen by the regenerate eye, nature is full of divine emanations. Edwards thought of these as images embodying ontological truth. The distinction between rhetorical and ontological images, or between tropes and types, we find carefully explained in Perry Miller's introduction to Edwards's *Images or Shadows of Divine Things,* a private notebook of some 212 entries.[38] To Edwards the sun, moon, rivers, trees, mountains, birds were not to be considered mere rhetorical tropes, common in the richly ornamented prose of the seventeenth-century Anglicans, but rather to be held as types that imaged or shadowed forth their spiritual antitypes. Nature is still nature, mutable and corrupt; yet its essence, Edwards said, is not in mutability or corruption but in the spiritual reality of which the sun and rivers and trees are the images. True spiritual sense discovers coherence in universal being, a divine agency in the world of historical and daily events, a divinity that shapes our ends. Everything becomes miraculous, the invisible enters the common world, and the unknown appears under historical circumstances. What other human faculty, Edwards asked, can decipher history and grasp the interpenetration of the divine and the human but that of the regenerate imagination? How else does the believer experience God's revelation—"the glory of God's works, both of creation and providence"? With true sense of the spirit the regenerate "will view nothing as he did before." Just as there is such a thing as "good taste of natural beauty . . . there is likewise such a thing as divine taste" in discerning spiritual emanations.[39]

Edwards held that imagination has more to do with discovery than with artistic creativity. Reality already exists, to be discovered by a gracious imagination. In the later Romantic view, imagination shapes a wholly new reality out of the elements first assimilated into its organic processes. This view supposes that the poet creates a new poetic image. But Edwards would have insisted that, because the poet's image was first taken from the visible world that he did not create, true creation belongs to God and the real image already embodies divine truth. In other words, divine creation precedes human creativity. All questions about what artists create are subsumed under divine creation, and aesthetic forms have importance only in relation to metaphysical reality. When, therefore, Edwards spoke of a new sense that goes beyond natural imagination, he did not mean the expansion of what Coleridge in the nineteenth century called the secondary imagina-

tion: that capacity to create something new out of what the
primary imagination first collected and sorted out. Edwards
thought of the religious imagination as the capacity to discover what already exists and, in the end, to apprehend the
full beauty and glory of the Creator.

To read Edwards's great sermons only for their literary
quality, as some recent critics have done, is to miss the fact
that in his concept of imagination words themselves were
accidental. What deserves special emphasis at this point is that
Edwards did not consider himself an artist nor did he consider natural imagination and poetic language as anything
other than the limitations of natural man. That art can neither
imbue the heart with religious affections nor adequately testify to these affections (both these points are basic in Edwards's thinking) brings to mind, for helpful comparison,
Kierkegaard's insistence that for religious experience the prerequisite is a renewed heart and a giving up of everything for
its sake. Kierkegaard believed that for the poet this means
relinquishing his art. Once a poet experiences religious vision, once he exists religiously, he either stops writing or
regards words as incidental, even as accidental. An eloquent
preacher, Edwards spurned the self-conscious artistry of the
seventeenth-century Anglican divines. For both men the
point of reference was God, not aesthetics. If, according to
Kierkegaard, a poet seeks through his natural imagination to
unite with the religious, "he succeeds only in establishing an
aesthetic relation to something aesthetic." If, on the other
hand, the poet through grace lives in a relationship to the
religious, if in truth the religious is the religious, then he will
know that true existence "does not consist of singing and
hymning and composing verses." Kierkegaard then noted
that if the poet's productivity "does not cease entirely, or if it
flows as richly as before, [it] comes to be regarded by the
individual himself as something *accidental.*"[40]

Again, Kierkegaard's emphasis rests on the point of
reference: if it is aesthetic beauty, then what is essential is
poetic productivity, not the mode of existence; if, on the
other hand, it is God, then existence within this relationship

is essential and words are only "accidental." Another way of expressing this distinction is to say that whereas art seeks to preserve, stabilize, and imbue with significance man's experience, religion shows the inadequacy of the human as an explanation of the way things are, and instead forces an alien vision upon man, undermines him, and finally discloses meaning only as he relates to the disclosure.

In order to discern the full sacramental dimension of the world, Edwards presupposed an imagination rooted in the power of the heart. It is in the prior experience of the redeemed heart that Edwards believed all the sources of imagination come together, and the first obligation of anyone who claims to envision the wonder of the invisible world and to speak of it is to affirm this original integration, the gift of grace.

Edwards is first and last a Christian theologian, not a literary artist. Furthermore, however much his theory of types resembles Ralph Waldo Emerson's later view that all natural things are emblematic of spiritual things; however close his ideas about spiritual sense seem to those of the Cambridge Platonists in England or the Antinomians in America; and however tempted one may be to transform Edwards's ideas on imagination into a theory of literary creativity, an all-important claim quickly dispels these similarities. The claim has to do with Christ as the final and ultimate mediator between human imagination and divine truth. According to Edwards, only through Christ can a person know the beauty of divine creation and providence. Only in this way can he truly see river, tree, and sun as types. Edwards rejected any suggestion that human imagination circumvents the fact of Christ. For, as Edwards wrote, unless Christ is seen first, "nothing is seen, that is worth seeing: for there is no other true excellency or beauty."[41] Only by this a priori condition can a person know anything more "than the devils do."[42] Holding to the singlemindedness of the Reformers, Edwards insisted that true sight comes only through the special impact which the Creator through Christ makes upon the heart.

Only as imagination functions within Christian revelation

did Edwards regard it as creative; only as imagination first discerns and then responds to the Creator did he say that a person can envision creatively. What he wanted completely clear is the distinction between Creator and creature. He never denied the importance of an active natural imagination, but its true activity originates in response to God. Therefore, only as human imagination envisions and creates from within the context of Christian revelation did Edwards think it could be trusted. Outside this context it is self-initiating, self-creating, and, by definition, arrogant, proud, sinful.

2

Puritan Faith, Romantic Imagination, and Hawthorne's Dilemma

I

Seventeenth-century New England "gave rise to more poetry, proportionately, than any other period in our history." This observation by Sacvan Bercovitch goes a long way to explain why increasing numbers of literary scholars are rediscovering early American literature. It can be said, of course, that thirty years ago Perry Miller also rediscovered the same literature. His task was to show that the intellectual terrain of seventeenth-century America, far from replicating a crusted European theology, was a complex mixture of ideas unmatched in rigor and dynamism by anything produced in subsequent American thought. Bercovitch and his revisionist followers, on the other hand, concentrate upon the Puritan as artist, and they strenuously elevate aesthetics from its previous subservience to theological dialectics. Bercovitch's *The American Puritan Imagination,* a collection of essays by twelve scholars, indicates the major theme in the "revaluation." Editor Bercovitch asserts that the Puritan legacy lies not in theology, logic, or social institutions but in the realm of the imagination. The interpretive clue to Puritan writing, he says, is its "imaginative substructure" and its "imaginative patterns." His concern is less with Christian theology and faith, less with the Puritan intellectual landscape, and more with metaphors, symbols, myth, and "mythico-historiog-

raphy." According to Bercovitch, the grand Puritan design
grew not so much from the doctrine of visible sainthood as
from a "gargantuan act of will and imagination."[1]

In staking his claim for the Puritan as artist Bercovitch
immediately runs the risk of perceiving one culture through
the alien eyes of another. In a major work, *The Puritan Origins of the American Self,* he interprets Puritan writing
through the eyes of later Romanticism, arguing, for example,
that Cotton Mather's *Magnalia Christi Americana* is not
Heilsgeschichte written from within the circle of Christian
faith but instead a "New World epic" in which symbolism
triumphs over typology, the person of John Winthrop
changes from a Nehemiah to a Prometheus, and Mather the
author evolves from a saint to a poet. Accordingly, Mather's
great work is informed by a gargantuan imagination rather
than a faith in redemptive history. The conception of a holy
hegemony took place in his imagination. In the end, Mather
was an artist, a symbolist, a mythmaker, who created rather
than discovered connections between secular and sacred history. Seeing in Mather the imagination of a symbolist rather
than the faith of a typologist, Bercovitch claims that "it is to
art that Mather's achievement belongs."[2]

The issue that will later confront Nathaniel Hawthorne
concerns the epistemological dilemma in the American experience between faith and imagination. That today's revision-
ists often fail to come to grips with the radical distinction
between these two ways of knowing leads them to neglect the
deep suspicions the Puritans themselves harbored toward art
and the imagination. In his definitive way Jonathan Edwards
reasoned that because imagination shares in the sinful nature
common to all persons, it remains limited and corrupt unless
infused with regenerative grace, in which case the important
truth rests not in imaginative art but in the initiatory role of
God and in the artist's response to *that* reality. Literary art
was seen as a species of rhetoric, a useful but limited means to
truth. In his classic summary of the Puritan "plain style,"
Perry Miller said that to estimate Puritan writings "from any
'aesthetic' point of view is approaching the materials in a

spirit they were never intended to accommodate, and is in danger of concluding with pronouncements which are wholly irrelevant to the designs and motives of the writers."[3] The key point concerns intentionality, including the larger theological matrix in which the writers understood their purpose. That this matrix presupposed what Miller called the doctrine of technologia meant (awesomely) that all created objects whether natural or "artistic" partake in a sovereign *theos*. Art has no privileged ontology, nor is the artist's imagination independent of God's will. Whether in poetry, history, narrative, sermons, or biography, the writer's intention adheres to the doctrine of means in which aesthetics serve rhetoric. Such writing has one main purpose: to convince the mind and move the passions regarding the revealed will of God.

In the seventeenth and eighteenth centuries when imagination became an instrument for perceiving nature—for making nature's sublimity commensurate with God and for making its laws synonymous with God—Reformed orthodoxy was seriously threatened. Even more portentous to it was the rise of Romanticism, which repudiated Christian supernaturalism, radical salvation, and the efficacy of faith. The Romantics in Germany and England accorded the imagination a redemptive power of its own, capable of transforming revelation into a secular theodicy—"a theodicy without an operative *theos*," M. H. Abrams has said—and capable too of incorporating the role of Redeemer. As Abrams points out, the Romantics undertook "to recast, into terms appropriate to the historical and intellectual circumstances of their own age, the Christian pattern of the fall, the redemption, and the emergence of a new earth which will constitute a restored paradise."[4] Their high argument rested upon the sovereignty of self, the mind and the imagination, all fusing into a free and creative soul knowing no limitations. The sacred fount was the self. Prayer was soliloquy. The poet for whom imagination was a means of grace perceived spirit in all things, became a liberating god, and heralded himself as the creator of a regenerative myth.

The "liberation" spelled the end not only of a covenant

theology but of another touchstone of Puritanism, namely, the idea of consent. What Edwards in *The Nature of True Virtue* (1765) had called "consent" to being meant a conscious decision to consent to God's sovereign will and divine election.[5] Consent led to a radically new propensity of the heart, an internal process consisting of key experiences and culminating in the acceptance of salvation. For the Romantic, on the other hand, consent meant an acceptance of the original self as wholly good. For Emerson and his German counterparts, it meant an affirmation of the self-determining, liberated human being; for Johann Fichte in *Addresses to the German Nation* (1807–8) it meant a "complete regeneration of the human race."[6] Contrary to the Puritans, who believed imagination functions within the matrix of revelation, including the created Word of scripture, the Romantics regarded imagination as independent and privileged, as the creative and saving power that restores original sublimity and harmony to beingness itself.

II

The two positions loom in striking contrast. To disregard this contrast or to interpret one position through anachronistic presuppositions of another may, in the end, be to join what was meant to be kept asunder. Between the claims of these two positions no nineteenth-century American writer struggled more than did Nathaniel Hawthorne. Risking a bizarre image, one thinks of Melville's description in *Moby Dick* of a whale whose two eyes must at the same moment examine "two distinct prospects," one on one side, the other in the opposite direction (chap. 74). For Hawthorne the distinct claims of Puritan faith and Romantic imagination reached far beyond aesthetics. Each epistemology presupposed fundamental theological differences precluding the use of one to interpret the other. Many readers have studied Hawthorne's hallmark of ambiguity: Yvor Winters called it "the formula of alternative possibilities," F. O. Matthiessen "the device of multiple choice," Richard Fogle "a pervasive quality of mind" symbolized by light and darkness. Instructive as these theories are, they fail to touch the deeper ground Hyatt Waggoner identifies as "art and belief." He stops short, however, by stating that Hawthorne's ambiguity is "a method of blurring the clear eye . . . a method, we may say, of avoiding clarity." As a caveat he adds, "but the kind of clarity that is avoided is the kind Hawthorne thought specious or irrelevant."[7]

The ambiguity is more than an artistic "formula," "device," or "method." Hawthorne stood between two opposing world views, two differing ways of knowing, two fundamental and conflicting interpretations of God, nature, and self. If ambiguity is said to be only an aesthetic quality in Hawthorne's writing, it does not encompass his dilemma between an extrahuman world and moral world principle on the one hand and the efficacy of the human mind and symbols on the other. Ursula Brumm has identified these two distinct positions. The first is "near Calvinism" and is carried on in what she calls the "semi-miraculous world of the romance"; the second has an "affinity with philosophical idealism and leads to poetic symbolism." Where then does Brumm place Hawthorne? As wavering, she says, between the two, "toying with both without making a decision." "He offers both without taking either seriously." Brumm acknowledges ambiguities that extend beyond the world of art; yet, she argues, these ambiguities in Hawthorne lack profundity because he "never wholly succeeded in uniting the two main constituents of his mind, the Puritan and the nineteenth century ones."[8] The problem here concerns a *Weltanschauung*. I have no argument with a critical assessment that shows ambiguity as part of Hawthorne's artistic method. But ambiguity may also describe a conception of the world and human existence. The lack of profundity that Brumm attributes to Hawthorne's ambiguity on this level is a judgment open to serious challenge.

The pull that Hawthorne felt from the side of nineteenth-century idealism informs his theory of art contained in the prefaces and the "Custom House" chapter of *The Scarlet Let-*

ter. Here one finds the familiar distinctions between actuality and the imaginary, matter and spirit, the quotidian and the ideal, as well as his theory of the imagination that unites these realms in art. The artist's imagination is seen as spiritualizing even the most commonplace things. It creates a "neutral territory" where the real and imaginary worlds come together, and where nature as perceived by the imagination becomes a vast landscape of symbols pointing to transcendent dimensions. From these notions Marjorie J. Elder concludes that "Nathaniel Hawthorne was a transcendental symbolist."[9] By analyzing his fiction in Emersonian terms she believes, furthermore, that a Hawthorne story is no less a "butterfly," no less an ideal embodiment of beauty, than was the mechanical one Owen Warland created in "The Artist of the Beautiful."

What Elder overlooks and Millicent Bell recognizes is the Puritan impingement influencing the way Hawthorne depicted his artist-figures. Owen Warland, for example, created a work of art in the butterfly, a "spiritualized mechanism," but as a human being Warland himself lived in the darkness of pride. His art does not regenerate his true nature, which Hawthorne describes as resembling "the frozen solitude around the pole."[10] Even though Hawthorne espoused Romantic theories of art and created fictional artists who consummated these theories in *their* own art, he himself kept a steady eye upon the sinister consequences when aesthetics displace ethics and specifically when the artist forgets that he is no different from any other sinner who thinks himself autonomous and his creations perfect. It is in the elusive category of intention (motive) and the a priori condition of the artist's all-too-human heart that Hawthorne's Puritanism worked its way with such potency as to make idealistic theories wholly ironic.

For Hawthorne the dilemma was not without its vocational ramifications. After leaving Bowdoin College in 1825 he put aside studying a profession, returned to his Salem home, and considered a life of art. "Year after year I kept on considering what I was fit for," he wrote to Richard Henry Stoddard in 1853, "and time and my destiny decided that I was to be the writer that I am."[11] What appears as resignation does not mitigate Hawthorne's turmoil in casting his lot with art. To Longfellow he confessed in 1837 that the decision had made him a captive of himself: he had entered a dungeon and lost the key. For the past ten years, he said, he had not lived "but only dreamed of living."[12]

This was the same year Emerson had warned that anyone choosing to live a life of the mind outside America's mainstream must expect poverty and solitude, hostility and loss. Of course Emerson was confident that such a person could become the "world's eye" and the "world's heart" ("The American Scholar") and, as a poet, could turn "the world to glass [and show] us all things in their right series and procession" ("The Poet"). Poverty would seem a small price for such promise. The Romantic saw himself as saved for some rare and special purpose, its worth heightened by the fact that "the incredulous world assails him with its utter disbelief."[13] Melville underlined these words written by Hawthorne to describe Owen Warland's sacrificial isolation. To Melville the heroic tone suggested a compensation, a certain private validation in one's suffering for art's sake.

The more significant dilemma, however, was not between art and public affairs so frequently delineated in American social history and literature. Granted that the profession of letters was a distinct break from the more respectable world of commerce, Hawthorne's tortuous problem concerned art as distinct from religion, imagination as distinct from faith. He was first and foremost an artist, but his great theme was what that calling held for the artist himself. In brief, Hawthorne cast his lot with art while being unshakably convinced that that choice came close to making him a sinner. As F. O. Mathiessen suggested, Hawthorne could not escape the thought that, in deciding to be a writer, he had made an "irrevocable choice" of evil fate.[14] His artist-figures embody his own haunting fear. Moreover, they embody all the sinister reflections that the mirror in many of his stories reveals to any good Puritan. These reflections tell far more about the artist's *temptation* to follow the profession of art than about the suffering that society exacts from those who do. Emerson had said nothing about this. As for Melville, who had underlined the words about Owen Warland's heroic isolation, he saved his heaviest markings for Hawthorne's "Monsieur du Miroir," a story about these deeper reflections that Melville called "uncertain" and "terrible."[15] Hawthorne's mirror had shown that common to all persons, including artists, is a heart susceptible to any temptation promising power over mankind and the gods.

At first this temptation is benign, as Hawthorne shows in "A Select Party," a story set in an airy castle, "a sort of no man's land."[16] To this place comes an assortment of guests who have escaped the world's perplexities in order to live in "the realm of Nowhere." In another story, "The Hall of Fantasy," the narrator finds himself in an edifice resembling some fantastic Moorish ruin, a place of "visionary atmosphere" to which people come not during waking moments but with "the universal passport of a dream." It is a "mystic region . . . above, below, or beyond the actual"; at its center is a fountain said to have "intoxicating qualities," and lining its halls are statues of artists with "meditative countenances and thoughtful, inward eyes." Not surprisingly, the narrator is drawn to these artists and their realm. Yet a tremor passes through him, and he is pleased to leave what he calls this "techy, wayward, shy, proud, unreasonable set of laurel gatherers." "I love them in their works," he says, "but have little desire to meet them elsewhere."

He looks back, however, tempted by the vision in which "the actual world, with its hard angles, should never rub against [him]," and tempted also by "a state in which Idea shall be all in all." He is beguiled by the artist's vaunted power to spiritualize actual life, to transform objects into symbols pointing to transcendental reality, to make the world transparent, to see all things in their right series and procession, and finally to become a liberating god. He dreams of being the embodiment of both the eye and what the eye beholds, both subject and objects. It is, of course, the Romanticist's dream that he can solve the old dualism by eradicating it through the redemptive power of the imagination.

The benign temptation to escape actuality presages the more seductive one to transform it according to one's vision. To slip from creature to creator, then to revealer of secrets denied the common man, then to prophet, and finally to demigod like Owen Warland, who would "turn the sun out of its orbit and derange the whole course of time," bespeaks a grand godlike, ungodly power. What matters is not that the Hawthornian artist is a eunuch (Clifford), a voyeur (Paul Pry and Coverdale), a dilettante (Kenyon), an "enwombed" bachelor (Warland and Fanshawe) but that as an idealist he is or has the potential for becoming a monster. He may think it his duty to observe with keen eyes even if the price is isolation and social opprobrium. However, the more sinister level is not the duty but the temptation to know life's deepest mysteries—that is, the temptation to be a puppeteer of someone else's soul, to remake and control the world, and to imagine oneself as its redemptive agent. Such power no longer pertains to the benign wish to escape the hard angles of the actual world. It is instead an "awful" power, and the temptation to have it is a curse.

Hints of these darker meanings appear in "The Prophetic Pictures," a story in which the artist-painter possesses the "awful gift" to paint not only the outward features but the mind and heart of his subjects. This gift of insight frightens those who, knowing the painter, look upon him with "vague awe." Walter and Elinor, the young couple whose portraits he paints, feel their privacy has been invaded when he is finished. In the years that follow, Elinor's gloom and Walter's fevered emotions have their terrible counterparts in the portraits, which, when scrutinized, reveal with uncanny accuracy what the artist confesses he saw from the beginning: "I have painted what I saw. The artist—the true artist—must look [trespass?] beneath the exterior. It is his gift . . . to see the inmost soul, and, by a power indefinable even to himself, to make it glow or darken upon the canvas." In Hawthorne's story the painter lives "insulated from the mass of human-kind," entertaining no aim, no pleasure, no sympathy except as it connects with his art. His heart resists the human warmth of Elinor and Walter, who continue to excite his fascination. He had "pried into their souls with his keenest insight," and so much of his imagination had been spent on his study of the couple that "he almost regarded them as his own." His subsequent paean to art voices dark irony: "O glorious Art! . . . thou art the image of the Creator's own. . . . The dead live again . . . there is no Past, for, at thy touch, all that is great becomes forever present. . . . O potent Art! . . . canst thou summon the shrouded Future? . . . Have I not achieved it? Am I not thy Prophet?" But of his own dark disorder, his preternatual acuity tells him nothing.

Hawthorne's artists think of themselves and their art as disconnected from the world of living human beings. In *The House of the Seven Gables* (chap. 11) Clifford feels an irresistible desire to send his "little impalpable worlds" (soap bubles of art) abroad from his window high above the street. Hawthorne himself wanted to create what he called in his Custom House chapter of *The Scarlet Letter* "the impalpable beauty of my soap-bubble," a self-contained world made out of the "airy matter" of his imagination. The artist Oberon in Hawthorne's "The Devil in Manuscript" exclaims, "I became all soul and felt as if I could climb the sky, and run along the Milky Way." But the desire to disengage from the actual world and, in Romantic fashion, to become a living soul carries its own moral indictment. To magnify the self is the self's own perversity. The ambiguity deep within Hawthorne's consciousness pertains to this problem of self. If selfhood is both the origin and the fulfillment of reality, then the self has already triumphed over any dichotomy existing between the actual and the ideal. Hawthorne suspected, however, that celebrating the triumphant self is triumphant irony. When Oberon awakens to the "nonsense" of his Romantic musings, he hurls his manuscripts into the fire of their true origin, the selfsame fire into which Ethan Brand hurls himself in a later story.

The Puritans took seriously the biblical image of hellfire. Whatever else it meant, it signified a state of existing apart from God. In Jonathan Edwards's memorable use of the image, natural man exists apart from his divine origin, as dangerously near to nonbeing as a spider dangling over a fiery void. The image reveals Edwards's concern not for the condition of spiders or man but for the relationship between sinful man and sovereign God. The relationship is at best precarious, kept intact only by divine mercy but subject also to divine judgment and dissolution. The image, which carries essential theological meaning, describes human nature as alienated from God, a condition, Edwards wrote, that "is *inherent,* and is seated in that *nature* which is common to all mankind."[17] Alienation also signified enmity against God and a disposition toward self-centeredness. The Puritan onlooker in Hawthorne's fiction suspected that the artist thinking himself triumphant in his sovereign selfhood and equating his creativeness with God's must be the most deceived of persons. The truth the one knew about the other was that self-love darkens the mind, hardens the heart, silences conscience, perverts religion, alienates man from the source of love and grace, and transforms him into a fiend. The artist's so-called lamp of imagination turns out to be nothing more than an *ignis fatuus.* In short, the flames into which Oberon casts his pages and Brand his soul are the flames of an all-consuming, all-destructive selfhood.

Whether Oberon is the "damned" author he fears or the "triumphant" one he calls himself is a distinction made meaningful in the paradox. True to Romanticism, Oberon hails the fire his imagination has conceived even while the same flames destroy his pages. His victorious "Huzza! Huzza!" anticipates Ethan Brand's panegyric, "Come, deadly element of Fire,—henceforth my familiar friend! Embrace me, as I do thee!" In severing the relational thread, the same which in Edwards's image confirms human dependency, Brand is forever damned. In his victorious independence is his disintegration, the ultimate irony of Romantic self-reliance.

Confronting Hawthorne as he stood between Puritanism

and Romanticism was the dreadful question of either/or.
One thinks of Melville's "equatorial" doubloon cast midway
up the Andes in a country planted on the equator, and the
fateful interpretation each crew member brought to the coin
that itself suggested the dividing line in a dualistic world. In
his essay "Experience" Emerson more serenely employed the
same equatorial image, that "middle region" where the cold
and lifeless world of abstraction and the other world of sensation can be brought together in imagination and poetry. For
Hawthorne the equator was the vertiginous gulf between human fallenness and the illusion of human perfectability. The
overwhelming question was whether to acknowlege the duality, reconciled through Christian faith, or to deny the opposition and herald the triumphant mind as synonymous with
infinity itself. The question juxtaposes the Puritan saint and
the Romantic artist. The frightful grandeur required to portray the former summoned Hawthorne's full genius in creating Arthur Dimmesdale. On the other hand, Hawthorne's
greatest fictive artists, even as they unite the two worlds,
stand damned in the paradise their imagination has created.

Hawthorne shows his hand when he requires art to contain
the soul of the artist. So far as art can capture the absolute, so
far must art also reflect its human origins in the heart of the
artist. That the Romantics hailed art as transcendental symbolism with its own teleological coherence followed from
their belief that the artist's nature was part of this same coherence. When Hawthorne, however, unites art with the heart of
the artist, an implicit Christian anthropology immediately
intrudes to posit a corrupt and sinful human being whose art
and all good works bear the same curse that marks their human origin. Art carries its own human birthmark. This is the
theological thorn implanted in the Romantic aesthetic. That
art disconnected from the heart is mere mechanical cleverness
is not Hawthorne's main point. The larger issue concerns the
sinful nature of the heart itself. However gorgeous the work
that issues from the heart and is used to cover it, as in the case
of Hester's scarlet letter, the work will bear the deadly mark
of its origination. When Hawthorne's artist-figures forget

this fact, an antiphonal chorus of mocking laughter ripples through the Puritan onlookers.

When the woodcarver Drowne (in "Drowne's Wooden Image") believes he has created a statue so perfect that it lives, he falls to his knees to gaze "with a lover's passionate ardor into the face that his own hands had created." For all the attractiveness of the Portuguese woman who served as Drowne's model, the greater seductive power is in the statue as a work of art. In calling the wooden object a "creature of my heart . . . my whole strength, and soul, and faith," Drowne believes he has created life and worships himself in it. The seductive agent is not the woman with "dark eyes" and "voluptuous mouth" but Drowne's own creative ego. Hawthorne did not need to destroy the woodcarver to warn that, as in the Narcissus myth, to adore oneself is to drown.

Using protective irony, Hawthorne has the "bigots of the day" as the ones who suspect the evil spirit in the beautiful statue to be seducing "the carver to destruction." One such bigot, "a Puritan of the old stamp," is certain that "Drowne has sold himself to the devil." A sensation of fear passes through others who, in seeing the wooden image as "something preternatural," ask, "Who and from what sphere this daughter of the oak should be?" Their perception of the artist's egotism serves as the story's contrapuntal echo, issuing as it does from Puritan bigots and blockheads. In an age of high Romantic fervor what better way for Hawthorne to shield himself than to have the town's laughingstock voice the fateful truth? They are the ones not deceived by the biblical serpent who promises, "Ye shall be as the gods." The serpent, whom Hawthorne calls a "bosom serpent" in another story, coexists with the artist's genius and loftiest aspiration. For Drowne this supreme moment was the "very highest state to which a human spirit can attain." But Hawthorne also adds that it was its "most natural state." In the adjective is the fateful curse.

For even at its highest state the human spirit is seen to be in bondage to its "natural" state, by definition fallen and devoid of regenerative grace. It therefore behooved saint and artist alike to go humbly, recognizing that unless the human soul is illumined first by the divine light as revealed in Christ, man in his natural state remains, as Edwards had said, "totally blind" and totally deceived. Changing his metaphor, Edwards had spoken of a "holy seed," a divine principle, a small thing like a grain of mustard seed, that comes into the heart, flourishes, and brings forth a new creature, one raised from the dead whose life now "is not only in a greater degree, but it is all new."[18] The distinction between old and new, death and life, blindness and sight is the same as that between natural imagination and regenerate faith. The former is a natural endowment common to all, the latter a spiritual endowment accorded the elect. The distinction is no less absolute than the Pauline one: "Whatsoever is not of faith is sin" (Rom. 14:23). The imagination of Hawthorne's artists projects the human and natural light of self. But Hawthorne's impinging Puritanism enforced a radically different theory of the imagination as a mirror reflecting the deep fantasies of a haunted mind and the dark emptiness of a natural heart.[19]

Hawthorne's scepticism regarding natural imagination did not elude Melville. On the one hand he admired Hawthorne's "No! in thunder"—the "no" spoken against any denigration of one's inherent and natural independence.[20] The artist courageous enough to stand against public judgment travels into eternity, Melville said, "with nothing but a carpet-bag,—that is to say, the Ego."[21] In "The Birthmark" Hawthorne had described the Romantic traveler in words Melville underlined. In this story the scientist Alymer, like a visionary artist, aspires mightily after the "gems which lay beyond his reach." What he sought was nothing less than the supernatural power to eradicate his wife's natural blemish, her birthmark. His ambition was evidence of his "higher nature," thwarted though it was by "the earthly part." In his copy of Hawthorne's *Mosses from an Old Manse* (1846) Melville underlined the whole passage that concludes with Hawthorne's reflection that every man of genius recognizes "the image of his own experience" in Alymer's.[22] Again in his copy of *Mosses* Melville triple-scored the heroic code in "The

Artist of the Beautiful": that the ideal artist "must keep faith in himself . . . must stand up against mankind and be his own sole disciple."[23] These were the same duties Emerson had spoken of in "The American Scholar."

On the other hand, when Melville came to write his review of *Mosses* a month later, he said little about "The Artist of the Beautiful" and settled instead upon "The Christmas Banquet" and "The Bosom Serpent." These two stories solicited the justly famous observation about the "other side" of Hawthorne's soul, "shrouded in a blackness, ten times black." Melville did not question whether this "mystical blackness" is merely an artistic device. The deeper issue concerned the "Puritanic gloom" lurking within Hawthorne the man: the "great power of blackness in him [that] derives its force from its appeal to that Calvinistic sense of Innate Depravity and Original Sin, from whose visitations, in some shape or other, no deeply thinking mind is always and wholly free." Speculating further about "this same harmless Hawthorne," Melville intimates that a "black conceit pervades him through and through," and that any bright gildings Hawthorne creates but "fringe and play" upon the edges of a darker truth known only in the heart.[24]

My purpose here is not to explore Hawthorne's "other side" as much as to examine his artist-figures, noting how their so-called higher state of aesthetic sensibility and imaginative authority contrasts with their abysmal moral darkness. The severed connection between aesthetics and morality or between art and the flawed heart becomes their moral undoing. This condition constitutes Hawthorne's great moral theme. By imperiling his Romantic artists, who disregard the truths of a Puritan heritage, Hawthorne brings to his own art a moral dimension lacking in the artistry of his fictive artists. As an artist he was preoccupied with morality. To remain both an artist and a moralist required that he use art as a theater, and that the touchstone of his artist-figures was to be their moral action. The artist whose highest allegiance is to art risks being Faustian; the moralist risks having his art barren and inconsequential. Hawthorne strove to defeat the evil nature of art with his moral intentions. He forced art to yield a good which would outweigh the dangers of cool detachment and the violation of another's moral sanctity. In the end Hawthorne rejects the artists Drowne and Warland, though not without engaging them, as it were, in a dialogue with himself in order to extrapolate his destiny in theirs. That he shuddered at what he saw stems from a Puritan consciousness that knows human achievement, however etherealized and perfect it may seem, to be only human.

Hawthorne's shudder has an even deeper cause than what he sees as the artist's moral chill, isolation, hypersensitivity, and monomaniacal aspiration. As a moralist Hawthorne fears that in the act of artistic creation he creates sin. For example, in Ethan Brand's highest effort (described with Rappaccinian overtones as "the bright and gorgeous flower, and rich, delicious fruit of his life's labor") Brand "had produced the Unpardonable Sin." He had *produced* it, *created* it: the sin of art itself. In his discussion of *The Scarlet Letter* James M. Cox argues in a parallel way that it was in "the artist Hawthorne's mind and heart, and not in some Colonial Forest, that the original act of adultery took place." What Professor Cox calls "Hawthorne's original sin" is, as I have suggested, "the sin of art itself."[25] It was this same insight that made Melville feel an inner diabolism in Hawthorne's *Mosses.* Hawthorne had made the devil a party to the work of art. He had raised the fiend out of New England demonology and had identified it with the creative process itself, with an illicit, destructive, enslaving power. Whereas this power makes the artist jubilant, it causes the moral man to tremble. The Romantic artist stands triumphant while a fearful peal of laughter from some far-off realm surrounds him. With irrepressible ecstasy Alymer looks upon his finished work, nothing less than his now peerless bride, and shouts, "You are perfect!" Brand also exclaims, "My task is done, well done!" Warland, beholding his butterfly, cries, "Yes, I created it." But at the same moment the mocking laughter pronounces its terrible judgment upon the two scientists, and a "secret scorn" towards the artist Warland arises from deep within Annie's consciousness.

The laughter goes unheard by Alymer and Brand. As for Warland, his pursuit had taken him beyond the region where Annie's moral scorn "might have been torture." Each has realized his loftiest aspiration, yet each is destitute of a moralist's shudder.

It was to make their listeners shudder that the Puritan divines spoke of sin in terms of fiends, serpents, demons, evil spirits—the same that fill Hawthorne's writings. Jonathan Edwards's injunction to the good citizens of Northampton to "search your hearts" echoed the opening words of Calvin's *Institutes:* "Without knowledge of self there is no knowledge of God."[26] To Edwards the imperative "Know thyself" meant, look beneath your "goodness," search the old wounds to the bottom so they can be healed. Without this inward scrutiny, without acknowledging inherent sin, any healing that supposedly takes place is vain and any regeneration outside Christ's radical atonement is a lie. For Edwards the fact remained that sinners had no such insights; they could neither rejoice in God's holiness nor shudder at their alienation from it. Only as they could shudder could they sense the dread of a sovereign judgment exposing their delusions, blindness, and death. Devoid of this sense they had no idea of the great drama raging between God and the devil within their soul, which was itself the prize at stake.

The artist-figures prize the marvelous gifts promised by the devil. Although a scientist, Hawthorne's Rappaccini describes these gifts to his daughter Beatrice: "to be able to quell the mightiest with a breath . . . to be as terrible as thou art beautiful." As Rappaccini looks upon his unearthly creations (first the gorgeous purple flower, then his transformed daughter and her lover Giovanni), his triumphant expression might have been that of "an artist . . . finally satisfied with his success." Nothing in Hawthorne's fiction shows human aspiration higher and at the same time more diabolic than that embodied in Rappaccini, who aspires to possess the "creative essence" with which he would recreate Beatrice and Giovanni into evil denizens of his garden. Whereas his prize is power, the devil's prize is Rappaccini.

The devastating indictment Hawthorne imposes upon artists and scientists alike is that they lack the sense of dread regarding their own malignant condition. They travel far out into ideality with their ego as their carpetbag but dare not travel the same distance within. They follow their high imaginative visions, fill the vastnesses of space and time, learn the cosmic secrets, and embody the divine creative spirit—all without a shudder. They are blind to what the dying Beatrice knows: "Oh, was there not," she addresses Giovanni, "more poison in thy nature than in mine?" The dying Dimmesdale makes the same judgment as he confronts his tormentor a final time. It is a profound moral judgment upon the Romantic ego, blind to the sin that Puritan consciousness beheld with fearful clarity.

"We must," said the Puritan divine Thomas Hooker, "look wisely and steadily upon our distempers, look sin in the face, and discern it to be full."[27] Melville compared this inner fury to a whaler's infernal try-works: a vast scalding pot of boiling oil surrounded by "snaky flames" that illumine wildly gesticulating harpooners with pronged forks—a "red hell" groaning and diving through "the blackness of the sea" (*Moby-Dick*, chap. 96). When beheld by Ishmael these fiendish shapes "begat kindred visions" within his own soul, leading to a shudder, woe, and madness. Jonathan Edwards also peered within to find his heart like "an abyss infinitely deeper than hell." Hawthorne's Arthur Dimmesdale, a Puritan saint and not a Romantic artist, found his to be a "pollution and a lie."

We may wonder whether Hawthorne heard the mocking laughter that surrounded his morally deaf artist-figures, and whether he felt an increasing desolation in art. The point is dimly inferred by the moral shadings of his narratives. The crux remains epistemological: how we know determines what we know, and what we know through imagination was, to the Puritans, only a shadow of what we know through faith. To remain in the world of art eventuates in a weariness and desolation of the soul, a hunger for another kind of food, more delicate, more internal, a food that to the Puritan poet

Edward Taylor imparts spiritual quietude passing beyond understanding and imagination. The unremitting truth Hawthorne may have heard in the Puritan laughter accorded little importance to the highest human achievements unless they are known and judged from a source of life and truth beyond them.

III

Hawthorne's juxtaposition of Puritan faith and Romantic imagination in *The Scarlet Letter* leaves a thin but profound line separating spirit and nature. To insist upon this line is not to ignore the complexity of the novel. The social, psychological, and aesthetic issues delicately intertwine with subtleties unmatched in American fiction. Yet we see how Hawthorne's own dilemma between the Puritan and the Romantic inheritance influenced the structure of his greatest artistic achievement.

The distinction reaches dramatic climax in the forest where Dimmesdale struggles with Hester's blandishments and his own consciousness of the weight, authority, and power of sin. On the one hand her argument carries the seductive Romantic promise to begin anew. "Give up this name of Arthur Dimmesdale, and make thyself another. . . . Up, and away!" (xvii).[28] She offered him "a new life" in exchange for the heavy doom he was expiating. "Let us not look back. . . . The past is gone!" (xvii). That Dimmesdale yields to her persuasion and to the Pelagian freedom of the will her argument rests upon accounts for a surge of physical strength that sends him leaping, thrusting, climbing, and plunging homeward through the forest. The new freedom also accounts for an inner "revolution" that releases an anarchic rush of evil impulses, inciting him to utter blasphemies to the trustful and innocent townspeople he meets on the way. For Dimmesdale, the flood of sunshine brought to light perverse predilections commanding him with terrifying authority.

Had Dimmesdale, then, kept a rendezvous with Hester or was it with the dark potentate? Or could it have been with one and the same? Frightful though Hester's promise of freedom was to Dimmesdale, as had been his sin of passion seven years earlier, even more terrifying now was the thought that such freedom was born not from natural passion alone but from a diabolical, heart-deep principle and purpose, seemingly confirmed by Mistress Hibbins's cackle that greeted the returning minister. Hester's argument, like a beautiful rose, had grown from a Romantic latitudinarianism. In this freedom of speculation, as in an untamed forest, she had lived "without rule or guidance." "Her intellect and heart had their home, as it were, in desert places, where she roamed as freely as the wild Indian in his woods" (xviii). Hester had remained her own inviolable self, independent and unrepentant, and she had looked "from this estranged point of view at human institutions and whatever priests or legislators had established, criticising all with hardly more reverence than an Indian would feel for the clerical band, the judicial robe, the pillory, the gallows, the fireside, or the church" (xviii). This was her strength; from it, now elevated to a principle of natural self-sufficiency, she promised Dimmesdale's rebirth and triumph. For his part, in succumbing he had reversed the Pascalian wager, fleeing not to God but to self—"as Hester would persuade me"—and then equivocally praying, "O Thou to whom I dare not lift mine eyes, wilt Thou yet pardon me!" (xviii). Not to be overlooked is the irony that their mutual flight would take them not into freedom but greater concealment. Thus they chose the Old World with its "crowds and cities" rather than the New World in the West.

In Dimmesdale's struggle the tormenting question concerns the nature of the self that Hester's beguiling arguments have helped to liberate and the flood of sunshine illuminate. With irony now compounded, he recognizes that freedom from moral principles and purposes actually enslaves him to the dark power of evil now exposed. Like his Romantic counterpart who cries, "Is Ahab Ahab?," Dimmesdale seeks to know what nameless, inscrutable power, what lord and master, now "haunts and tempts me thus?" (xx). "Am I mad?" he cries, "or am I given over utterly to the fiend?" The question comes down to: Is Dimmesdale Dimmesdale? "Did I," he asks, "make a contract with him [the evil potentate ruling Hester and himself] in the forest, and sign it [like a baptized harpoon] with my blood? And does he now summon me to its fulfilment, by suggesting the performance of every wickedness which his most foul imagination can conceive?" (xx). Is the assertion of self-will only the assertion of larger powers ruling the self?

Although Dimmesdale's new gospel of Romanticism takes him perilously close to Ahab's fate, nothing in American literature makes the contrast between the two positions more vivid than the death of these two radically different giants. Gripped by the power whose source is "hell's heart," Ahab defiantly seeks to kill "for hate's sake" the very thing he is tied to, whereas Dimmesdale praises the God of Judgment and acquiesces to His will. The one goes to his death according to the conception of how he should, the other according to the Almighty's conception. What had taken place in Dimmesdale's study after his return from the forest Hawthorne carefully veils, except to suggest that the tormented minister, torn by opposing claims, recognized that his rebirth in the forest had been fraudulent and his so-called transformation, which had "stupefied" his blessed impulses, had brought him into fellowship with "the world of perverted spirits" (xx). When we see him again, on his way to deliver his rewritten Election Day sermon, he appears not as the inspired self-asserting rebel who had burst from the wilderness but as one whose strength now "seemed not of the body" (xxiii). Hawthorne's stylized ambiguity suggests this new energy "might be spiritual," imparted to the saint "by angelic ministration" (xxii)—indeed, a strength from heaven, a gift of grace, empowering Dimmesdale to preach with mighty eloquence, to clasp the hands of Pearl and Hester, to mount the scaffold with them, to make public confession and reveal his own stigmata, to escape Chillingworth's evil grip, to find a freedom radically different from the one earlier dreamed of, and, in short, to do what he had withheld himself from doing

for seven years and, in the end, to die "the death of triumphant ignominy" (xviii).

To Hester this clergyman making his way in the procession
to the meeting house and finally to the scaffold was a stranger, empowered with a spirit not of her natural world and
with a strength that left him "utterly beyond her reach" (xxii).
A different transformation had occurred, one in which she
had had no part and in which "there could be no real bond
betwixt the clergyman and herself" (xxii). So "completely"
had he left behind their mutual world that she "could scarcely
forgive . . . thus much of woman was there in Hester" (xxii).
Bitterly resentful, she reached out with cold hands and
"found him not" (xxii). Instead she found Mistress Hibbins
standing close beside her and sharing, in a communion of
knowledge, the recognition of Dimmesdale's mysterious re-
moteness.

The radical breach had been prefigured in the forest. On
one side of the brook stood Hester in radiant beauty, her
stigma cast aside. On the other side played little Pearl in
seemingly the same natural element. Immediately perceiving
the brook, however, to be "the boundary between two
worlds," Dimmesdale fatefully tells Hester, "thou canst never
meet thy Pearl again" (xiv). For all the interwoven likenesses
joining mother and daughter, we are made aware that little
Pearl stands in her father's world too. Fixing her eyes steadfastly upon him while preternaturally sharing his consciousness of guilt and divine judgment, Pearl makes her father's
hand move, as if involuntarily, to his breast and causes Hester
to feel in some indistinct way "estranged" from her child.
From this different world across the brook Pearl points to
Hester's discarded letter, and with "a singular air of authority" requires it replaced. Only then will she acknowledge
Hester as her mother. What might be called the Dimmesdale
side in Pearl sharply contrasts with the endowments originating from her mother, the difference ultimately signifying that
between a Puritan and a Romantic consciousness.

The depth and center of the minister's heart where his ultimate transformation occurs is deeper than where even Chillingworth can probe. Neither physician nor artist can get to this deepest region, a fact acknowledged by Chillingworth at the moment of the minister's public confession, and implicitly acknowledged by Hawthorne himself, who stays his probing at the study door of Dimmesdale's dark night of the soul and allows his readers no entry even into the meeting house to hear the minister's pentecostal words. We are not privy either to Dimmesdale's solitary encounter with his God or to his pulpit eloquence, its unheard language more spiritually pure, as it were, than that which, if heard, would have "clogged the spiritual sense" (xxii). What Hawthorne cannot depict whether through psychology or imagination is the core of Dimmesdale's being, the essence of which is not the totality of his natural capacities but the spirit whose energy derives from a Creator separate from one's own creatureliness. Thus Dimmesdale's new spiritual sense, described in traditional language as regeneration and accounted for experientially by Christian saints from Paul and Augustine to Luther and Edwards, is a change in the nature of the heart itself, wrought not through works including acts of penance but through the miraculous gift of grace. This experience was Hawthorne's task to depict, an undertaking most artists have eschewed. The extent to which Hawthorne succeeded is measured by the credibility of certain incredible paradoxes.

Hawthorne's frequent use of ambiguity is not to be confused with his recognition of paradox. Ambiguity can be a distancing strategy to suggest multiple meanings, whereas the very contradictory meanings of paradox constitute its truth. He knew that to Puritan saints Christian truth was paradoxical, not ambiguous. As a religious sceptic, an artist might enjoy the luxury of ambiguity, but as a believer confronting religious paradox the saint suffers the tumult of faith. Hawthorne's challenge was to create the Puritan saint who personified the paradoxes while at the same time inhabiting a world of his creator's ambiguities and sometimes wild imaginings. Dimmesdale is foremost a Christian believer struggling with the religious meanings of his life. Notwithstanding his complex psychological condition, which includes guilt, hypocrisy, libidinous fantasies, and archetypal wanderings, his life is necessarily a crisis of Christian paradoxes that culminate when submission is his freedom, weakness his strength, ignominy his triumph, and death his life.

No less revealing than Ahab's final utterances are those Dimmesdale spoke to Hester, showing him the Christian antithesis to the Romantic hero. Woefully conscious that alienation from God ("the law we broke") led to a spiritual alienation from each other ("we violated our reverence each for the other's soul"), the minister yet trusts God's mercy. Such trust is not heroic confidence or endurance, natural gifts both, but a Christian hope different from earthly hope. So too is his faith different from earthly understanding, and his religious love (far beyond Hawthorne's means to show) different from earthly love, which orthodoxy suspects as being merely self-love. The triumph surpassing understanding is the spiritual resolution Dimmesdale brings to the most offensive of Christian paradoxes: "He [God] hath proved his mercy, most of all, in my afflictions" (xxiii). Thoroughly Pauline in his theology, Dimmesdale interprets his "burning torture" and his death as the inevitable prerequisites to his salvation: "Had either of these agonies been wanting, I had been lost forever! Praised be his name! His will be done! Farewell!" (xxiii). The words echo those of St. Paul: "I take pleasure in infirmities . . . in persecutions . . .: for when I am weak, then am I strong" (2 Cor. 12:10). The ultimate extension of the paradox ordains that in dying we live, in having nothing we yet possess "all things" (2 Cor. 6:9–10). Hawthorne's handling of the spiritual event requires Dimmesdale's physical death to herald typologically the *dying to* the old natural self. The life-giving spirit, emphatically not a direct heightening of the natural life, is a new life, with death necessarily separating the old and the new. To live anew is first to *die to* the natural gifts of understanding, public triumph, and ego in order to receive the spiritual gifts of faith, hope, and love. In his "Conclusion" (xxiv) Hawthorne calls Dimmesdale's death a "parable" by which the minister taught his parishioners that the holiest persons are those who recognize the inconsequence of their merit and the divine mercy that looks down upon them. The parable, which postulates two worlds, becomes an experience in knowing death in the one world and life in the other, and a beginning in the end.

Admittedly Hawthorne withholds the new vision from the minister, who must leave unanswered Hester's plea, "Tell me what thou seest?" (xxiii). Yet Dimmesdale alone owns the paradox of mercy in affliction, triumph in agony. Little did the townspeople know of his private ignominy, even less did they understand his election day sermon about it, and now in his public confession they know nothing of his private triumph. The reversal is as complete, radical, and contradictory as only the paradox can embrace.

Visible sainthood was an impossible commission that Puritan clergy consigned themselves. The suspicion arises that the laity *needed* such visibility in their clergy so as to have in their midst a model of Christian sanctity. Without something close at hand to verify their easy faith and security, the people otherwise would be left with intolerable uncertainty about the marks of faith. For the clergy, visibility exacted a terrible price, namely, hypocrisy and guilt. The subject pervades Jonathan Edwards's three great treatises: *Distinguishing Marks of a Work of the Spirit of God, Some Thoughts Concerning the Present Revival of Religion in New England,* and *Treatise Concerning Religious Affections.* It asks the saint, "Can you heal others without being healed yourself?" Or the more excruciating question, "Am I indeed healed at all?" Dimmesdale's visible sanctity satisfying his public role made him only the more tortured by a private conscience that discerned, again with Pauline awareness, "the contrast between what I seem and what I am!" (xxii). Dimmesdale's unremitting self-examination left him profoundly insecure. Had he been devoid of conscience—had he been "an atheist" or "a wretch with coarse and brutal instincts"—he might have found peace long before (xvii). But he belonged to a long tradition of introspective achievement in Western Christianity, starting with Paul's Epistles and Augustine's *Confessions,*

and developing in the Middle Ages with the kind of penitential practices of flagellation, fasting, vigils, and visions that
Dimmesdale himself desperately adopted. He was the kind of
Christian who turned in on himself, absorbed by the question
of how God (or Satan) was working in the innermost individual soul. Such introspective conscience reached its
theological climax in the Reformation and its secular climax in
Freud. For Dimmesdale, introspection inspired the great ser-
monic theme of the universal brotherhood of sin and the
private knowledge that "his heart vibrated in unison with
theirs" (xi). Had he believed himself healed or needing no
healing, he would have been least fit to heal others, for he
would have separated himself from them. Instead, he
identified his predicament with theirs, and used his election
day sermon as "the complaint of a human heart, sorrow-
laden, perchance guilty, telling its secret, whether of guilt or
sorrow, to the great heart of mankind" (xxii). That his au-
ditors regarded the sermon as the minister's crowning public
triumph, which nicely corroborated for them his professional
eminence, only betokened their introspective want.

The hypocrite we see in Dimmesdale is nothing more than
he saw in himself, but far more than his parishioners saw in
themselves. He was the one who alone felt the universal throb
of sin, and he the one who traveled the Christian introspective journey. His inner turbulence is the lifelong and chronic
crisis of one who seeks answers to the questions of how to
escape corruption in living and how in death to give meaning
to life. Such a person Erik Erikson finds exemplified supremely in Martin Luther, "the first Protestant at the end of
the age of absolute faith."[29] It was this giant Reformer who,
in freeing conscience from totalitarian dogma, underwent the
precariousness of faith, the consciousness of duplicity between doing and being, and the terror of introspection. Erikson quotes Luther's words that presage those of the Puritan
Dimmesdale: "I did not learn my theology all at once, but I
had to search deeper for it, where my temptations took me.
*Vivendo, immo moriendo et damnando fit theologus, non in-
telligendo, legendo, aut speculando:* A theologian is born by

living, nay dying and being damned, not by thinking, reading, or speculating."[30] Like Luther's search, Dimmesdale's
"constant introspection" brought anguish to his inmost soul
but no purification. Neither penitential acts nor self-loathing
could effect a radical transformation of the heart. Nevertheless, to shudder at his sinful condition did indicate an
uneasy conscience, the first step on any pilgrim's way.

It is well to consider the shudder wracking Dimmesdale
when he faced himself as a "pollution and a lie." Insisting
upon self-scrutiny, the Puritans meant to shatter any compla-
cency that insulated them from all that is mysterious. Their
demand for painful wakefulness resembles Rudolf Otto's assertion that if man could only shudder he would know what
having the fear of God means. For "shuddering," Otto said,
"is something more than 'natural,' ordinary fear . . . it implies
that the mysterious is already beginning to loom before the
mind, to touch the feeling."[31] Natural man, however, is destitute of such a sense, and sin and salvation are only so many
tedious arguments. Deluded by the feeling of self-sufficiency,
he has no sense of hell, no sense of alienation.[32] Like the
Reformers, Edwards believed that self-sufficiency, fostered
by liberal Arminianism, protected the unregenerate from
sensing the depths of sin and the power of evil that, according
to Paul Tillich, had been at "the center of Luther's experience
as it was in Paul's."[33] Unlike many of his eighteenth-century
contemporaries, Edwards believed that sin was true of all
humans, past and present; and in his preaching he sought to
make his listeners conscious of it at their present moment: to
awaken them to themselves, to have them apprehend hell as
separation from God, and to expose them to their own condition. On the level of everyday experience he interpreted in-
sensibility first as self-sufficiency, pride, smugness, and, secondly, as the apathy that leaves one's soul (like that of
Prufrock) etherized, unaware of life's contingencies, be-
numbed to insecurity. The message was intended to burn into
the core of present existence. It called for perilous introspection whereby foundations are shaken and human beings
shudder. It warned that unless persons first see their fractured

condition, they remain outside the saving knowledge of divine things. It heralded the shudder as the prelude in the drama of salvation and wholeness.

Dimmesdale's shudder opens him to a world of spirituality that includes human sin and divine judgment. He alone hears the shrieks of guilt he sends abroad from the scaffold while the town sleeps, and he alone beholds the immense letter *A* spanning the night sky in judgment upon all earthly mortals. Hawthorne's ambiguities concerning the blazing phenomenon and its meaning rest upon the event as a revelation addressed only to Dimmesdale. A public servant, he resides in a world of Christian mysteries invisible but to spiritual consciousness. A Protestant smitten by the compulsion to verify Christian truths experientially, he perceives the world as a cosmic stage where both God and man have their awesome parts to play. He and Melville's Starbuck, who eyes the doubloon, share a Christian cosmology, but the minister's consciousness of it extends far beyond what Starbuck knows—and into a different world from that of Hester.

To say this is not to discount Hester's agony. For her, the scarlet letter carried its weight and its torment. But its reality was something society imposed upon her from the outside, a punishment decreed by the world's law and a humiliation enforced by its citizens. The letter left untouched her deeper nature. To remove the letter was simply to undo its clasp, and the stigma disappeared as easily as the letter. Thus "with the stigma gone, Hester heaved a long, deep sigh, in which the burden of shame and anguish departed from her spirit. Oh exquisite relief!" (xviii). Even to have worn the letter as an act of penance for seven long years had "wrought out no repentance" (xv) because, for Hester, there had been so sin, therefore no divine judgment, and nothing to repent. For her the adultery had had its own consecration, accorded by her Antinomian independence: the "world's law was no law for her mind" (xiii). Indeed, what was "most to be repented" was not the adultery at all but her marriage to Chillingworth, including the fact "that she had ever endured, and reciprocated, the lukewarm grasp of his hand, and had suffered the smile of her lips and eyes to mingle and melt into his own" (xv). What festered in her consciousness was not guilt for having broken a law, whether God's or society's, but resentment for not having been true to her own feelings, which she regarded as pure and sacrosanct. Also festering was hatred towards Chillingworth for having "persuaded her to fancy herself happy by his side" (xv). She regarded his successful persuasion as "a fouler offense" than any he had committed since, even his demonic quest to destroy Dimmesdale's soul. Her hatred of Chillingworth is fierce because she had exposed her weakness to him. Blindly she charges him for having betrayed her, forgetting that she too had wronged him in her adultery. As Chillingworth was to remind her, "between thee and me, the scale hangs fairly balanced" (iv). Theirs is a mutuality of betrayal, deepened by their respective capacity to hate. We see no stricken conscience marking Hester's life, no fear and trembling, no dread of God's ordinances or prayer for his mercy. Hers is a "haughty smile," a "giddy independence," an "impulsive and passionate nature," and a lofty pride that appears to separate her from her would-be judges and tormentors. In time Chillingworth comes to see in little Pearl's nature the part that includes her mother's inheritance: "There is no law, nor reverence for authority, no regard for human ordinances or opinions, right or wrong, mixed up with that child's composition" (x).

However, in Hawthorne's portrait of Hester, aloof in her imagined independence, are the dark shadowings of a threefold heretic, subject to the judgment of the Puritan community and also to the three persons closest to her. First, a Pelagianism that would absolve her from inclusion in corporate original sin and Augustinian predestination bespoke her heretical freedom to initiate in the forest the change that brought her a surcease of anguish and, to her consort, a new vigor and hope. The transformation, wrought through "the minister's will and Hester's will" (xx), supposedly proved their capacity to effect salvation without divine assistance. Fraudulent though Dimmesdale later realized the conversion to have been, it is Chillingworth who enunciates what to the

Puritans was the truth, namely, that a "dark necessity" rules the human way. "My old faith," he earlier had said to Hester, "comes back to me, and explains all that we do, and all that we suffer" (xiv). He understood that, contrary to Pelagianism, no individual has the freedom of will to choose not to sin, and no individual unassisted by grace has the power to pardon one who has fallen. This is Chillingworth's insight, as orthodox as that of any Calvinist. "By thy first step awry," he continued, "thou didst plant the germ of evil." The implication is clear that no puny will of hers or his can deflect the iron way of fate. Her adulterous deed, by which she had wronged her husband, fatefully had planted within him the seeds of vengeance that now transformed him into a fiend. Still, he added, her betrayal and his vengeful monomania are not to be thought of as singular sins of individuals who are free and therefore answerable and accountable. Their sins, he said, are "typical"; they partake as "types" in the corporate sin of mankind from Adam to the present and carry predestined consequences, an interpretation which again is unequivocal Calvinism.

Pearl is the one who refutes her mother's Antinomianism. This second heresy was the same for which the Puritans had expelled Anne Hutchinson, whose legacy in Hester's Boston is the rosebush still alive by the prison door, symbolic of Hester's sovereign spirit standing in repudiation of law *(nomos)*. Such freedom dangerously sanctioned a person to live apart not only from religious legalism but from all law, including the accepted standards of Puritan morality. This was the freedom Hester asserted when she removed her scarlet letter and "flung it into infinite space" (xix). With this symbolic act she declared, "I undo it all, and make it as it had never been!" (xviii). The significance of this act goes beyond the mere freedom from magisterial law that she enjoys for a brief moment. For the Puritans, Antinomian freedom dangerously liberated one from the creeds of the faith which, though such creeds could never capture the faith, were necessary to unify the faithful into a communion of saints. The gravest danger, however, was the nature of the freedom sym-

bolized in Hester's removal of the letter. It was the freedom
of her natural self to be a law unto herself, radically different
from the freedom given a regenerate self. As Hawthorne
knew, the difference is theologically crucial. Christian orthodoxy argued that regeneration brings the freedom, for example, to do good to those who hate us, to bless those who
curse us, to pray for those who abuse us, etc. This kind of
freedom, the orthodox said, human beings do not naturally
possess. Instead they are born self-centered, self-important,
self-concerned, and, accordingly, grow up self-indulgent and
self-righteous, apart from grace. They are not by nature free
at all but slaves of self-will. The Calvinist view mocked as an
illusion the freedom Hester granted to herself and Dimmesdale. It was the freedom associated with heretical Antinomianism that Pearl shattered in demanding of her mother:
"Come thou and take it [the scarlet letter] up!" (xix). Take
your foreordained place within the world's law, she was in
effect demanding.

   Still another heresy springing from orthodox Calvinism
was what the Puritans called Arminianism, after Jacobus Ar-
minius of Holland and his followers, who, in attacking the
doctrine of absolute election, emphasized the importance of
works as a means to divine election. Many there were who
recoiled from the concept of God's arbitrariness in choosing
whomever he would, despite the good works accomplished
by the aspiring. The controversy figures into Hester's effort
to persuade the suffering Dimmesdale of his worthiness. Citing the good he does among his parishioners, she assumes that
his penitence is "sealed and witnessed by good works." But
the minister answers, "As concerns the good which I may
appear to do, I have no faith in it. . . . There is no substance in
it! It is cold and dead, and can do nothing for me! Of penance, I have had enough! Of penitence, there has been none!"
(xvii). Clearly his acts of penance have not wrought a penitent
heart. True to his orthodoxy, Dimmesdale believes that his
acceptance is by faith alone (sola fide), quite apart from any
"works." Finding no merit in the use of works to influence
God's election, he reveals his theological position to be in

accord with a Protestant orthodoxy that rejected the Catholic
idea of satisfaction or acts of atonement as part of penance.
Contrition and confession, yes, but acts of penance he considered bound up with the idea of merit and indulgence which
presumably cheapened the grace of God and obscured the all-
sufficiency of Christ's atoning act. As for good works,
Dimmesdale scorned their value when they originated from
an unregenerate ("polluted") soul. Only when motivated by
gratitude for God's saving grace, only when performed in
willing obedience to him, only when empowered by the love
of God and not of self were they to be called good. It was his
hard and relentless indictment against Arminian do-goodism
that also exposed Hester's spiritless charity in sewing coarse
garments for the poor when "no genuine and steadfast penitence" was in it, when nothing made her feel that she belonged to their condition, and when she "stood apart from
moral interests" more in repugnance than in sympathy. Even
though her works for others displayed patience and even
martyrdom, "she forebore to pray for her enemies" lest the
words became a curse (v). Even though the scarlet *A* came to
signify Able, there was no penitence when she returned to
Boston years after she had forsaken it with Dimmesdale's
death. She returned still devoid of repentance and revelation,
still a woman of strength but not of joy.

The fragile enjoyment that flowered during her earlier
years in Boston derived from her art of needlework and the
powerful imagination behind it, not from sewing garments
for the town's poor. The latter cost "a real sacrifice of enjoyment"; it represented only a gratuitous "idea of penance" (v).
Her needle brought her no closer to the world of want than it
brought her to that of wealth and power when she embroidered ruffs and gloves for the magistrates. Her art had
quite the other effect of taking her out of ordinary relations
with the townspeople and "enclosing her in a sphere by herself." Art expressed her independence. So "artistically" had
she embellished the scarlet letter—"with so much fertility and
gorgeous luxuriance of fancy"—that the splendor far exceeded "what was allowed by the sumptuary regulations of

the colony" (ii). Fullest play of her free imagination came in the embroidered gold-threaded "fantasies and flourishes" (vii) of Pearl's crimson velvet tunic. The creative energy expressed in both letter and garb originated from the same natural impulse expressed in the forest before the novel opens and embodied in the child. Beautiful as her needlework was, something wild and unruly lay behind it, corresponding to the passion underlying Hester's voluptuous and elegant beauty and also the defiant waywardness beneath the "deep and vivid tints" of Pearl's beauty. The letter *A* and its imposed signification of Adultery Hester transformed into Art, a proud and independent act.

The deeper hues of beauty reflecting a certain wildness in both mother and child are also the hues that grow from out a heart of sin. Here we find Hawthorne's central insight concerning art and the Romantic imagination. Whether the outgrowth be the rancorous weeds covering some moldering grave or a magnificent thing of beauty wrought by an artist's hand, an inexorable similitude exists between the object and the heart beneath, tainting even the richest beauty with corruption. Even in what appears most sacred, like the blessedness of mother and child, the taint can be found.

For all the open independence of her soul, linked neither to heaven's God nor earth's humanity, Hester was confined in ways she sometimes only faintly recognized. Deep within her wellspring were strange alliances she was unable to renounce. One was with Chillingworth, upon whom she fixed a gaze so intense when he first emerged from the forest that, for her, "all other objects in the visible world seemed to vanish, leaving only him and her" (iii). Despite the overt cleavage brought on by her adultery, she shared with her husband an artist's fascination for what lies beneath people's appearances. Hester's "new sense," an endowment attributable to her wearing the scarlet letter, gave her knowledge of the hidden sin in other human beings. The thrill was most "electric" when she recognized the disparity between outer appearances and inner realities in minister, magistrate, and maiden. Chillingworth, of course, selected Dimmesdale as his single object for reasons of revenge, but he was fascinated enough that he would have pursued his investigation of the minister's disparity "were it only for the art's sake" (x). The alliance between artist and scientist extends still more deeply into their shared delusion when first they married: for Chillingworth, that intellect compensated for his physical deformity, and, for Hester, that a marriage to which she brought no love would bring to her "a new life" in some romantic Continental city, "ancient in date and quaint in architecture" (ii). At its deepest level, the alliance binds not only their mutual betrayal but their common wrong against the unsuspecting Dimmesdale. Chillingworth's fiendish guile does not exonerate Hester's culpability in keeping from the victim the knowledge of his tormentor's identity. Abjuring her responsibility was "the iron link of mutual crime" (xiii) that not only left the minister at the mercy of the physician's malevolence but so disorganized and corrupted the patient's spiritual being as to send him to the brink of madness. "Such," indeed, "was the ruin to which she had brought the man" (xvii). "Do with him as thou wilt!" she had earlier confided to her misshapen ally. In truth, both Chillingworth and Hester had discovered some deadly source of strength within the deep surrounding forest, he from secrets learned from its savages and she from dark intimacies shared with some vague potentate, some Black Man, some Evil One.

The blurry association that Hawthorne creates between Hester and this dark presence achieves no further clarity than the ambiguity arising from the association between her and Mistress Hibbins. In this shadowy alliance Hester instructs the witch to explain to the Black Man why she (Hester) will not attend his merry forest company of a night, but later the same Mistress Hibbins invites her to ride together some night "to see thy father" (xxii). On election day the two together discern Dimmesdale's strange transformation; together they stand arrayed in mutual magnificence, Hester with her emblazoned letter and the witch with "triple ruff, a broidered stomacher, a gown of rich velvet, and a gold-headed cane"; and together they expel an aura that distances them from others in the crowd.

These alliances serve to mock Hester's independent self. They suggest a thralldom too profound to break, a chain too binding to annul, unless, in some gracious way, reborn eyes perceive the chain as a "magnetic chain of humanity." To recognize humanity in its corporate sinfulness and oneself as interlocked in this universal condition is the first glimpse of a new and different freedom. On one side of Hawthorne's dilemma is this Christian paradox that only twice-born eyes can reconcile. On the other side stands the independent Romantic self for whom once-born vision is complete.

To view Hester as the centerpiece and heroine, as twentieth-century readers increasingly do, is to lessen the tug between Romantic imagination and Puritan faith. Such a view diminishes the significance of Dimmesdale's internal conflict between these polarities, a conflict that serves as the novel's dramatic locus and projects not only Hawthorne's dilemma but that of his time. Moreover, to shift one's conclusive attention to Hester is to forget the scarlet letter Dimmesdale bore, the same mark we all bear within. By the end of the century William James would come to regard Dimmesdale's condition as that of a "sick soul," more a psychological aberration than a spiritual crisis. For the modern audience, no longer subject to transcendent imperatives, Dimmesdale's conflict carries little urgency when seen alongside Hester's "problem," namely, selfhood vis-à-vis social imperatives. Today's compelling issue is less salvation or damnation than acculturation that requires a compromised self. As against such compromise, a residual Romantic bias affirms independence and finds in Hester this selfsame strength. But hers is a different conflict from Dimmesdale's; hers is one in which questions concerning human existence are asked in a world devoid of any divine tug.

3

Ole Rölvaag: Space, Time, and Kierkegaardian Dichotomies

I

All America heard Hester's enticement to Dimmesdale, "Up, and away! . . . Let us not look back. . . . The past is gone!" Her declaration caught the prevailing mood of a nation bent upon making a new American personality that would fulfill its natural endowments and coincide with its national mission. In his 1844 story, "Earth's Holocaust," Hawthorne fancied how the old philosophies along with their encrusted traditions and institutions would be destroyed in a purgative apocalypse to make way for the new impulses, spoken of by Holgrave, the young reformer in *The House of the Seven Gables* (1851): "Shall we never, never get rid of the Past? It lies upon the present like a giant's dead body" (xii). Let us, he proclaims, "decently" bury it and get on with building a new world. The summons was raised to exaltation in Whitman's "Song of Myself" and Emerson's "American Scholar." Thoreau intended the response to be a ritual of purification, a sloughing off of old accretions in order that natural man awaken to his true self. The cleansing was not of the Puritans' natural man but of the conventional man, in order, precisely, that the natural man could be truly born. For Emerson, Thoreau, and their Romantic disciples the dichotomy was not between nature and divine spirit, man and God, sin and salvation, but between the natural and artificial

79

(conventional), the new and the traditional, the individual person and the social mass. R. W. B. Lewis correctly identifies New England transcendentalism as "Puritanism turned upside down."[1] Thoreau marched to the music he heard, but it was not as totally different as he announced it to be. It was the music of his own age, and, as Lewis observes, it sent Thoreau "in a direction *opposite* to St. Paul" and away from Hawthorne's dark cavern of the human heart.[2]

But the story of nineteenth-century America remains untold if immigration plays no part. What of the millions who came bearing the old accretions and who were forced to find their New World in American cities or on its Western prairies and the mountains beyond? Far from representing an organic transition from the Old World or an evolutionary stage in a larger process, the immigrant experience was a radical break, leading to the trauma of a divided heart, a wound that the American promise never healed except in the vicarious assimilation immigrants felt in their children who, Americanized, moved beyond their parents' orbit.

Immigration itself represented a collision between old and new, often leading to the radical juxtaposition of an inherited Christian orthodoxy and a new Romantic freedom and myth. In Ole Rölvaag and John Muir this collision serves as an important and useful example. Both men were Old World figures bearing religious traditions, of Norwegian Haugeanism and Scottish Calvinism respectively, and both, according to popular interpretation, supposedly sloughed off their burdensome inheritance to enjoy American rebirth that accompanied the Western apotheosis.

As a novelist, the Norwegian Rölvaag made the mind and heart of the immigrant his foremost subject. At times he eyed the mythical garden as the place where the immigrant annuls his past and fulfills his previously envisioned future. At other times, however, Rölvaag shifted his attention away from the garden and toward the ominous wilderness, a more compelling metaphor for suggesting what it meant to be a stranger in a strange, new world. Unlike the garden, the wilderness evoked brooding darkness where storms of nature corresponded with those of the inner self. In depicting this inner world Rölvaag shared in the tradition of artistic expressionism, which extended from Goya, Gauguin, and Van Gogh to the likes of Chirico, Chagall, and the Picasso of *Guernica*. Rölvaag's compatriot, the painter Edvard Munch, also depicted this inner realm where self-revelation and emotional intensification brought forth frightening, neurotic, obssessive concerns associated with love, sickness, alienation, and death. Nothing in Munch's canvases terrifies more than the image of fear, the unreasoned fear we experience in nightmare, seen in *The Scream*, painted the same year (1893) that Rölvaag nearly lost his life in a Norwegian storm at sea. The painter's long, rhythmic strokes convey the echo of the scream into every corner, every segment of the picture, transforming the earth and sky into a gigantic world of fear.

The purpose of placing Rölvaag alongside his compatriot Munch is not to establish attribution but to suggest a similar spiritual context. In this same setting can be heard the voice, sometimes the scream, of Knut Hamsun's fictional characters, and the tremulous words of novelist Johan Bojer's protagonist Per Holm in *The Great Hunger:* "Now it was that I began to realize how every great sorrow leads us farther and farther out on the promontory of existence. I had come to the outermost point now—there was no more."[3]

The promontory is the boundary between two worlds: between native land and alien country, Old World and New, accepted belief and radical questioning, limitation and infinite desire, sanity and madness. Living on the boundary is perpetual crisis, spoken of in Rölvaag's opening sentence of *Boat of Longing:* "The place lay on the sea, as far out as the coast dared push itself, and extremely far north, so far, in fact, that it penetrated the termless solitudes where utmost Light and utmost Dark hold tryst."[4] The promontory is the place of fateful decision, the place where young Rölvaag, now determined to be an emigrant, stood alone on the Lofoten pier and watched the boys who had brought him to it sail home in the same boat he had been so fond of. Standing on the pier and staring after them until they disappeared behind Skarvholmen on the other side of the fjord, he felt at that moment as if "a door closed within me and a room was locked forever."⁵

In 1896 the twenty-year-old Rölvaag stepped beyond the promontory and headed for alien country. He later remembered how as a newcomer, making his way on foot from Elk Point, South Dakota, to his uncle's farm deep in the darkness of night, he had lost his way at a crossroad, and, not knowing his directions, how he "would gladly have traded a stormy night on the Vestfjord for this summer night on the prairie." "It seemed so ironic," he reflected, that he should die of hunger and exhaustion "right here in the promised land."⁶ When Rölvaag came to write *Giants in the Earth* some ten years before his death in 1931, he knew his ailing heart would not allow him many more years to live. More to the point, he felt himself still standing on the promontory, still gazing at the world left behind and also at the engulfing darkness lying ahead. Rölvaag was still the immigrant—"to the end of his days a spiritual denizen of Nordland"⁷—but one who now was intent upon transforming his painful internalization into spiritual and artistic truth. He had found his governing metaphor in the wanderer alone in space, another Ishmael. The measure of his success would come in the fictional character of Beret who, locking her past inside a trunk, stood a stranger in the American wilderness, a place of crisis where light and dark held tryst and where the terror beyond the promontory filled the earth and sky.

Thus it is instructive to see how this old world figure, Ole Rölvaag, played his part in the great new Romanticism of the American West. Admittedly his arrival from Norway's far northland in 1896 was too late to make him a frontiersman, and his settling five years later in Northfield, Minnesota, represented a kind of eastward movement from his South Dakota farm work and preparatory schooling. But his imagination roamed over the Western prairies, inhabiting them with a new kind of giant, the archetypal pioneer who embodied the transcendentalist vision.⁸ Rölvaag was never to relinquish the vision. Two years before his death he continued to speak of Norwegian-American pioneers as "The Vikings of the Western Prairies," and in his last public appearance, a month before his death in November 1931 at the age of 55, he addressed a Chicago audience on the western epic, quoting Whitman's lines in "Pioneers! O Pioneers!":

> All the past we leave behind,
> We debouch upon a newer mightier world, varied world,
> Fresh and strong the world we seize, world of labor and the march,
> Pioneers! O Pioneers![9]

Although the American world Rölvaag had stepped into in 1896 had voices telling of ominous things to come, forebodings to which Rölvaag was not deaf, his powerful immigrant voice harmonized with songs American Romantics were singing. To say this is definitely not to tell the full story of Rölvaag's imaginative life and writings, but there is no denying that the superb character of Per Hansa in *Giants in the Earth* (1927) stands tall among the heroes of America's New Direction.

Early in the nineteenth century Alexis de Tocqueville had noted that the eyes of American pioneers "are fixed upon another sight."[10] It was, of course, the future, not the past. The house and barn, the village, the town, rising from the open land, represented a triumph over what had been, and signaled what was yet to be. By now, the story has been told countless times, and the historical events have been transformed into superhuman terms like American Adam, Manifest Destiny, Chosen People, The Garden, Virgin Land. For Rölvaag's pioneers, evidence seemed close at hand that their kingdom had come.

Implicit in Rölvaag's novel and the whole epical westward movement is a view of history relatively new in the consciousness of our civilization. In analyzing this perspective Robert Heilbroner explains that until a few centuries ago the dominant view of historical time had been the past, not the future. Early people did not look ahead for the ideals and inspirations of their existence, but sought them "in their origins, in their ancient glories, their fabled heroes . . . real or fancied."[11] With modern consciousness came a new orientation in which people set their goals in what is to come and dreamed of a world they would make. Confirming the dream was their apparent power to control nature and ignite upheavals and revolutions leading to fundamental changes in social, economic, and political life. According to Heilbroner, the belief dawned during the Renaissance that human beings could effect changes that would loosen the grip of the past upon the present. A few centuries later America came to symbolize the realization of that belief.

The underlying Romantic enticement was to live separate from history and the past—to escape what Mircea Eliade has called the "terror of history" by abolishing time and linear history, fusing historical events into timeless myths, identifying human life with nature's eternal repetition, and finding some kind of archaic existence within it.[12] In this tenor American Romanticism conceived the American as being firstborn, a new Adam, to make and shape things as he would. In a similar vein Frederick Jackson Turner theorized in 1914 that a "forest philosophy" had accounted for our values. According to his well-known theory, our American ideals were not brought to Virginia in the *Sarah Constant* nor to Plymouth in the *Mayflower* but were born in "the American forest," radically apart from European origins or "germs."[13] What happens, however, to intellectual history if the present environment be all was only one of many questions Turner's theory failed to answer. Unlike a Poe or a Melville, Turner gave little thought to the appalling possibility that in freedom, autonomy, and sovereignty were to be found the germs of human madness. The notion of history as only or largely the product of our free volition, as something we "make" in a virginal land, has proved too simplistic. Such a notion brushes aside the heritage of our common condition, the ambiguity of events, and especially the mystery (destiny, force, necessity, fate, providence) that lies outside our power to understand and control.

The more deeply one reads in the immigrant Rölvaag the darker is the underside of his Romanticism and the more ironic the "new life" of his heroes. The view embodied in a Per Hansa and celebrated by Rölvaag in his public utterances is challenged repeatedly by Per Hansa's wife, Beret, as well as by Rölvaag's own deeper musings. The challenge sprang from a Christian view of history that opposes both the myth of the eternal return and the Romantic celebration of the expanding and ultimately nonhistorical self. Rölvaag often vacillated between the two positions, affirming Romantic optimism on the one hand but also responding to the Christian view containing the implicit question that Kierkegaard posed: "Is it possible to base an eternal happiness upon historical knowledge?"[14] This is a different question from the one Eliade asks: "How can the terror of history be tolerated?" For Eliade the answer is resignation, transcendence, or nihilism, whereas the answer for Kierkegaard is Christian faith rooted in historical events. To Kierkegaard historical truth is a given condition from which he speculates as to whether the historical can be intersected by an eternal consciousness and still remain historical. Although the question exists within a Christian orientation, it is the question that structured Kierkegaard's insistence that Christianity is the religion of historical man. Accordingly, the Christian sees himself as part of a linear continuum. So squarely and so completely does he live within time and history that to strive to transcend them through the power of will, ego, and mind is to strive to become what one is not and to annul what one is, to forget that humans live in time before they live as spirits in the eternal, and to reject the paradox that only by living in the one can they inherit the other. The Christian believes that history, although linear and finite, has been intersected at a point identified as the Incarnation, making history, in spite of its apparent absurdities, providential and eschatological.

II

The two views of history stand in conflicting juxtaposition. Per Hansa lives in one, Beret in the other, and Ole Rölvaag, their creator, suffers the anguish of straddling both. This is a tension extending more deeply into his consciousness than the ones frequently cited as the social and cultural disloca-tions experienced by Rölvaag and his fellow immigrants. The perils of rootlessness and the cost of settlement, two of Röl-vaag's major themes, have ramifications extending beyond the consequences delineated by sociological or psychological criticism. To identify Rölvaag's devotion to the Norwegian heritage of his people on the one hand and, on the other, his concern about their future in America—to identify these as the "two fixed poles" between which Rölvaag's thoughts were "forever oscillating" is to leave untouched a deeper level of his consciousness.[15] Even to argue that the grand theme in his fiction is the transition which his people achieved rather than the ordeals they suffered[16] is still to come short of the level that questions whether a person exists as autonomous or dependent, whether he lives in or out of history, and where the fateful consequences lead from each respective locus. It is on this level, represented by Rölvaag's paradigm of *space* and *time*, that one begins to see the novelist's deeper conscious-ness, troubled over the dark truths of existence.

In the measureless oceans of space surrounding Per Hansa the inhabitants seem as "specks" living and moving in this awesome expanse. Faraway covered wagons appear as tiny "white dots" lost and totally vulnerable. The solitary wagon that creeps into sight on one occasion *is* lost, its occupants hungry and disoriented, the mother deranged from the fam-ily's wandering over the prairie for nearly six weeks and from having buried their youngest out on it somewhere. The ex-hausted father explains to Per Hansa, "One night he was gone—just as if you had blown out a candle."[17] Per Hansa saw for himself the condition of Kari, the mother: how she had ridden inside the wagon, her wrists tied to the handles of the great chest, her face drawn and unnatural, the scene re-sembling a crucifixion. Such things happened to puny mortals who left behind the ancient landmarks of their fathers and ventured into infinite space. Some were lost, others de-stroyed, still others returned to the familiar markings before it was too late, yielding in the raw fight against retributive doom. As the father of this forlorn family muttered, "I can't tell how it happened; Fate just will it so. . . . It isn't any use to fight against Fate" (311).

In this setting Per Hansa's great ego emerges. He embodies a power that stands against fate, is more immense than fate, attends and antagonizes fate. The imagery is as Emersonian as is the confidence imbuing this epical pioneer. In his essay "Fate" (1852) Emerson juxtaposed the great contraries of freedom and fate, liberty and necessity, the individual and the "laws of the world." He depicted man in this gigantic confrontation as the master, the one who somehow appropriates fate for the strengthening of his own will, so that in the end fate is what Emerson calls "Beautiful Necessity," its beauty being in its resistance to the person who, in mastering the resistance, reaches his grandest fulfillment. Fate is what the human will has not yet mastered. For Per Hansa space is what he has not yet conquered, destiny is what he has not yet fulfilled. His strength lies in his ego, and this is enough, so it seems, as he stands against the sky, not as a speck like the other wanderers but as a mountain bulking large and elemental, ready to withstand any invaders, whether the Irish or the trolls. He stands as a giant pioneer, larger than life, driven by some inexplicable source that his awed neighbors sometimes suspect as being witchcraft. But who is to say, as Hawthorne asked, that such demonism is not part of the selfsame ego?

Per Hansa disregarded Beret's mother and father back in Norway who had pleaded with him not to take their daughter away, offering him all they had—boat and fishing nets, home and barn—if only he and Beret would stay. "But Per Hansa laughed it all aside!" (218). Alone on the prairie Beret came to understand what the laughter had meant. It had betokened "west-fever," an intoxication that left Per Hansa and the others with "bewildering visions" of a land rich in corn and wine.

> Human beings gathered together, in small companies and large— took whatever was movable along, and left the old homestead without as much as a sigh! Ever westward led the course, to where the sun glowed in matchless glory as it sank at night;

people drifted about in a sort of delirium, like sea birds in mating time; then they flew toward the sunset, in small flocks and large—always toward Sunset Land (220).

Does west-fever imply a soaring, skylark spirit or does it augur ambiguous undulations and a sinking downward into darkness? Rölvaag hints at an important distinction here. Depicted in Per Hansa, the human will is sovereign and free to create its own world. The self is not lost in space but "fillest, swellest full" its vastness, as Whitman sang in "Passage to India." Ultimately the self fashions the cosmos and becomes one with it. When Per Hansa speaks repeatedly of "my Kingdom," it is not merely the few acres of land, the house, barn, and crops that he envisions but the power to possess and control these things, to claim ownership of them, and eventually to see them and all nature as extensions of his being. Freed from time and its impingements, he interprets space as total possibility. By contrast, Beret thinks of herself as an inheritor, and all people as indebted to the past and rooted in it, dependent upon it for their well-being. She looks upon reality not as spatial extension of ego, imagination, and vision but as an already created world in which humans take their place as creatures. Insofar as they create anything, they do so within a creation already given and with origins deeper than what the mind imagines. An all-too-human Norwegian immigrant, subject to loneliness and shattered hopes and terrible fears, Beret cares little about an American Adam in a mythical garden.[18] A complex interplay of emotions registers longing and regret in every joy, and reminders of the past in every present moment. Rölvaag's genius is his understanding of this other kind of immigrant mind that modulates and clouds the soaring dream. Rölvaag characterizes Beret in this way, too sensitive to rest easily with illusions of conquest and too steeped in the nuances of her heritage to exchange them for a new Eden. Accepting her place in a world where time and history govern, she shudders at the consequences for those who do not accept their limitations.

Her sense of terror stems from at least two causes. One is that of space, the empty desolation of the prairie. A similar terror grips the beholder of Robert Frost's woods and Melville's ocean. To the best American writers has come the consciousness of an infinite void beneath the apparent benignity of nature. For Beret "no road led back" (32) from this desolation; she saw herself and others astray and abandoned, not as pilgrims but as strangers far from home, ritual, order, and history. The solitary ego created no sufficient counterforce to keep the terror at bay. Indispensable is the reunion of families and the "ceremony" that ensues after their own number, earlier astray on the prairie, rejoin the others. The occasion is celebrated by a white cloth spread on the raw ground and all taking food together. Without the intervening protection of community and its ways, including its traditions, rituals, relationships, and moral guideposts, the terror of space would prove overwhelming. For example, what brought relief to the deranged Kari, after six terrible weeks in trackless space, was the sod house of Beret and Per Hansa.

> She entered a *cozy room* where *things were as they should be;* she felt the warm presence of *folk who had dwelt here a long time.* She took in the whole room at a glance—*table* and *benches* and *stools;* a fire was burning in a *real stove;* a *kettle* was boiling; wet *clothes* were hanging on a line by the stove, giving out a pleasant, familiar odor; and there actually stood *two beds*, made up with clean bedding! The *sense of home, of people who lived in an orderly fashion,* swept over her like a warm bath (314, italics mine).

Beret perceived that unless Kari regained her bearings by living once more with reference to time, place, and other persons, the deranged woman would be lost forever. Beret covered the windows for the same reason; she kept out what was larger than life. Hers is a human orientation, like the one that almost melts the hardened heart of Melville's Ahab just before he takes his final step into the infinite: that single precious moment when the staggering giant speaks to Starbuck—

"Close! stand close to me Starbuck; let me look into a human eye; it is better than to gaze into sea or sky; better than to gaze upon God" (*Moby-Dick*, chap. 132).

Time and the human element give meaning to the old family Bible that Beret's grandfather had handed down to her. "This book had been in her family many generations; her great-grandfather had owned it before her grandfather; from her it should pass on to Store-Hans" (184). The same meaning applies to the old churchyard she remembers in Norway where many of her family lie: "two brothers . . . and a little sister . . . her grandparents, on both her father's and her mother's side, also rested here, and one of her great-grandfathers. She knew where all these graves lay. Her whole family, generation after generation, rested there" (222). Most important for Beret is the family chest that had belonged to her great-grandfather; its barely visible words, "*Anno 16——,*" indicate it had been in the family even before his day. Desperately she looks to it for her security, her link with the past. More than this, the chest signifies the past itself, the place of her origin. Its religious importance as a communion altar later in the novel deepens its historical signification.

I have said that Beret's sense of terror grows from two causes. The first is to stand outside the community, including its moral landmarks, and to behold "these infinities" (182). The second is to see the change in Per Hansa as he takes up this very position. One thinks again of Melville's Pip who, after witnessing the crew's revelry following their pledge to join Ahab in his hunt, prays to be preserved "from all men that have no bowels to feel fear!" (*Moby-Dick*, chap. 40). More than anything else, Pip fears the fearless man. Something happening to her husband strikes terror in Beret, not because he might lead them into disaster but because, in achieving his new kingdom, he will sacrifice his human heart for a more heroic one that knows no fear and, in its isolation, trusts only itself. Melville's little Pip intuitively knows that worship is the rightful act when one beholds the infinite; even the wild crew, in seeing the corposants, intuit this rightness and act accordingly. But Ahab's way is to defy the infinite's claim, and it is this defiance that strikes panic into Pip. Similarly, Per Hansa was possessed by an "indomitable, conquering mood . . . a driving force so strong that she [Beret] shrank back from the least contact with it" (41). She sees in Per Hansa's expanding self-trust a subversion of the doctrinal *sola fide*. Beret fears her pioneer husband has become his own lawgiver and self-declared *exemplum* of truth.[19] In *The Concept of Dread* Kierkegaard called this solipsism "demonic shut-upness," a denial of all order and reality that would make a person accountable.[20] Scorning the landmarks of his past, Per Hansa destroys the literal ones of the present—those planted on his land by other immigrants. Heedless also of the Indian burial ground his land encompasses, he will have no ghosts of the past to deflect his course. "This kingdom," he reiterates, "is going to be *mine!*" (35). Beret fears anyone who sets himself to realize all possibility at any cost. Frightening though the infinite prairie is to Beret, even more terrifying are its supernatural emanations that sometimes resemble a gigantic and menacing face, the face of evil that she thinks may be her husband's double (32).

III

The visit to Spring Creek of an unnamed minister, the first to appear since the founding of the community, intersects the repetitive flow of days and seasons, and deepens the dichotomy in the novel. To explore this still lower level, which only the term religious adequately describes, it is necessary to consider in some detail Rölvaag's own religious ideas and at least one of their sources. Important though it is, the source is only briefly alluded to by Rölvaag's biographers, Theodore Jorgenson and Nora O. Solum: "it is tempting to believe that he may have been under the influence of the Danish philosopher, Sören Kierkegaard." They add: "Rölvaag read Kierkegaard, presumably quite early in life and with greater diligence after he had begun to specialize in Norwegian literature." Beyond noting that Rölvaag could hardly have studied and taught Henrik Ibsen without know-

ing "Ibsen's spiritual kinsman in Denmark," Jorgenson and
Solum say little else, except to point out that Rölvaag's use of
the diary as a literary device in *Letters from America* (1912)
resembled Kierkegaard's same technique in *Either / Or.*[21]

In a brief sketch John Heitmann, a lifelong friend of Rölvaag, recalls that while still boys on the Norwegian island of
Dönna he and Rölvaag read aloud together Kierkegaard's
Either / Or.[22] Later as a lonely twenty-year-old immigrant in
Elk Point, South Dakota, Rölvaag was befriended by the
Reverend P. J. Reinertsen, who helped him learn English and
whose library, consisting mostly of theological works including those of Kierkegaard, young Rölvaag devoured. His dis-
cussions with Reinertsen were important not only for Rölvaag's intellectual growth but also for the admiration he was
later to show in his fiction for the typical pioneer minister in
the West who, Rölvaag thought, should be well-grounded in
such theological writers as Kierkegaard.[23]

That Rölvaag came under the influence of the great Danish
thinker is reasonable to assume. Common to both men was
not only a Scandinavian culture but also a certain system of
regulative ideas that shaped their lives. Moreover, a profoundly religious spirit as well as a deep restlessness
intensified the paradoxes they found in life. Hating what was
trivial and passionless, both men probed into the depths of
existence and dared to contemplate divine meanings. Furthermore, a spiritual grandeur coupled with a brooding darkness
mark Rölvaag's *Giants in the Earth*, as these same qualities
distinguish the vast themes in Kierkegaard's *Either / Or, Fear
and Trembling, The Sickness Unto Death, The Concept of
Dread*—the very titles evoking a sense of awe. More
specifically, both men equated the matter of choice with what
it means to be human: to choose is to acquire selfhood. Kierkegaard explained that "choice itself is decisive for the content
of personality."[24] Not only does he immerse himself in the
thing chosen, but also in the act of choosing or in what Kierkegaard calls "choosing to will," a person chooses to be. To
avoid choosing, to deliberate, to postpone is to fall short of
real personhood.

These were some of the ideas Rölvaag encountered in Kierkegaard's *Either/Or*. In varying degrees these same ideas inform Ibsen's plays and, especially, *Brand,* in which the clarion theme of "all or nothing" is surpassed only by the imperative of choice itself. About the play, set in Norway's forbidding mountains, Rölvaag said it chilled him to the marrow of his bones. "But that chill did something for me. It made me run on and on and on."[25] In his lecture notes about Ibsen's play Rölvaag wrote: "We fairly reel as we peer into the depths that he opens. . . . He seems to wage the despairing struggle of a strong soul against the riddles of eternity, which he feels that no soul can solve. His [Brand's] is a Prometheus-like combat . . . a Titan's heaven-storming struggle to find light." Affirming his own oneness with the spirit of Brand, Rölvaag continues: "Of his motto 'All or Nothing' I have nothing but good to say. . . . The motto is in perfect harmony with the teachings of Christ."[26] Determined to pursue this theme, Rölvaag, as it were, set his own face to go up to Jerusalem. The essential point to reiterate concerns the primacy of choice made with the whole inwardness of personality, choice that transcends "multifarious" alternatives and "immediate" consequences (these are features of "aesthetic" choice which Kierkegaard condemns as being no choice at all) in order that the person reach the ethical level where the absolute either/or is between good and evil and where, as seen with Rölvaag's Per Hansa and with Ibsen's Brand, the consequence of choosing is irrevocable.

Existence in terms of either/or was Kierkegaard's answer to Hegel's idea of synthesis which includes and also reconciles the contradictory ideas of thesis and antithesis. This notion of mediation was as abhorrent to Kierkegaard as was the timorous postponement of choice itself. To Kierkegaard mediation meant compromise. Whereas the concept of either/or is "the pass which admits to the absolute" and "the key of heaven," the concept of both/and, Kierkegaard said, is "the way to hell."[27] With equal fervor Ibsen's Brand declares, "Compromise is the way of Satan."[28] The devil that Brand saw was the spirit of moderation, luxury, ease, and moral laziness among the dull and cloddish townspeople. As for Rölvaag's Per Hansa, a heroic superiority shines forth in his great decision to face the unknown West. In his choosing to will, a choice which lifts his existence into the ethical, he finds his selfhood. That his son Peder Victorious embodies compromise suggests something of a diminished if not withered sense of being.

Heroic in his choosing, Per Hansa is fallen in his choice. This is the paradox informing great tragedy. Choice and the dreadful possibility of damnation are inseparable. Moreover, if choice bespeaks the freedom to choose, then even the most heroic self-attainment is doomed. Grand as Per Hansa was in choosing to build a "new kingdom," equally darksome was his pride and, in Christian terms, his sin for presupposing total human initiative. His choice in the end did not lie merely between two cultures or between tradition and freedom but between human initiative and divine imperative. What Per Hansa never came to realize was that the problem of life was not the discovery of an ideal or the power of will whereby to achieve it, but rather the redirection of the will away from self and toward the ruling sovereignty of God. Ultimately, choice must give way to faith, which is a matter not of will but of grace.

Giants in the Earth is far more than a national epic of immigration and the westward movement. Its underlying issue is salvation, and Per Hansa is as far from it at the end of the novel as he was at the beginning. That he achieved Kierkegaard's ethical level of choice raises him to the stature of a tragic hero. But of Kierkegaard's religious level of faith he knows nothing. At the heart of the matter is the question of will, basic in Pauline and Reformed theology and best spoken of in America by Jonathan Edwards. Will is as its strongest motive is. Prior to will, by which a person chooses, is a more fundamental cause identified as motive.[29] According to one's motive, so he chooses; as he chooses, so he acts. But again the paradox arises: the free act of choice is already determined by a prior motive that among the unregenerate is always that of self-love. The credo of natural man is always "Not Thy will but mine be done." Per Hansa leaves no doubt as to whose will is sovereign for him and whose kingdom he seeks.

The whole question of the religious level of existence, which I believe Per Hansa's wife Beret reached but he himself did not, requires further examination of Kierkegaard. *Either/Or*, the longest of his works, records his struggle and ultimate victory over the so-called aesthetic world view. But it was never on the achieved ethical level that Kierkegaard meant to rest.

Beyond the aesthetic and the ethical questions Kierkegaard inquired specifically into what the Christian way of life demands. Included among such writings as *Fear and Trembling*, *Repetition*, *The Concept of Dread*, and *Concluding Unscientific Postscript*, all of which treat this religious level of life, one particular work deserves special notice. This is Kierkegaard's *Purity of Heart Is to Will One Thing*, the first of his *Edifying Discourses* from 1847. The subject of this discourse concerns the biblical text from James 4:8, ". . . purify your hearts, ye double minded." As for the question, "What is it to will one thing?" Kierkegaard examines what men customarily seek in this workd—pleasure, honor, riches, power—and then goes on to argue that to will any one of these things is necessarily to be double-minded. In none of these things can there be said to be one eternal and essential thing. "Only the Good is one thing in its essence," Kierkegaard says. Only the good is not subject to the rule of change, by which he means "the change of death."[30] Purity of heart, therefore, is to will the only thing that in its essence *is* one thing, namely, the good that is God himself. To will anything else is the despair of double-mindedness.

But even to will the good may be double-mindedness if the prior motive is what Kierkegaard calls the "reward-disease," or if it is the fear of punishment, or, once again, if it is the self-centered wish to "score the victory" rather than to serve God. The stern command to purify the heart is not only to will the one good that is God but, says Kierkegaard, "to do all for the Good or be willing to suffer all for the Good."[31]

That Rölvaag read *Purity of Heart* seems certain, as evidenced in his speech of 18 March 1907 to the Luther League. On the St. Olaf College faculty for two years, he was now probing ever-deeper philosophical ground. In this speech entitled "What Is It to Will One Thing?" he uses the same text from James's Epistle and follows Kierkegaard's argument point by point.[32] "If," Rölvaag said, "we are going to will one thing, a thing that is complete, then we must will that which is good, because only that which is good can be willed in this way." Everything else in the world is "in its essence not one." Like Kierkegaard, he argues that "neither indulgence nor wealth nor power nor honor is one in [its] inner being." Thus to will anything of this world, Rölvaag said, is to be "two-minded." As for the question of prior motive in a person's willing the good, Rölvaag admonishes that goodness willed out of the hope of reward or the fear of punishment shows merely the failure to understand that to will the good is always to will life itself. If the mind be single, then one's self will be full of the light that is God's essence; if double, the self will be lost in the darkness that is death. For both Kierkegaard and Rölvaag the level of concern extends to religious faith and purity of heart. It is on this religious level that the ultimate issues of life and death, salvation and reprobation must be met.

In another of Kierkegaard's works, *Fear and Trembling,* he retold the story of Abraham and Isaac in order to contrast the ethical world view of either/or with the religious imperatives that take priority over all ethical principles. On the abstract and ethical level of right or wrong Abraham's sacrifice of Isaac was patently and universally wrong; but God's sovereign commands, not bound by any set of principles or laws, were made singularly to Abraham and required of him the suspension of the ethical in favor of the teleological—because the *telos* involved was God. According to Kierkegaard, it was not that Abraham balanced the claims of ethical principles against the claims of God and then chose the latter, but rather that as between the two Abraham believed in the latter. With purity of heart he took the leap of faith. In *Fear and Trembling* Kierkegaard presented a Lutheran denunciation of ethical moralism, which had substituted abstract principles for God's authority. The faith of Luther, of Kierkegaard, and finally of Rölvaag's Beret in *Giants in the Earth* ruled out both a moralistic interpretation of God's action and a self-willed choice as the way of human response. God's design was clearly more than a system of ethical ideas requiring choice on the part of his people. Instead, his was a glory requiring faith through grace.

Throughout Rölvaag's novel the tension between Per Hansa and Beret corresponds to these two Kierkegaardian levels of existence. We notice that despite Per Hansa's "indomitable, conquering mood" and what at times appear to be his superhuman achievements against the elemental forces of earth and sky, a note of apprehensiveness like some faintly minor key surfaces repeatedly in Beret's moods and words. This presence, of course, has psychological causes related to her loneliness on the desolate prairie, her deep need for tradition, and her guilt for pregnancy out of wedlock. But Rölvaag intends something more in the spiritual desolation Beret feels as she joins Per Hansa in his work and vision. As the farms all around get finer and the barns bigger, the certainty of divine judgment overwhelms her. To Beret the psychological cost in leaving their fathers' homeland is nothing when compared with the spiritual cost in forsaking their fathers' God. In Per Hansa's pride she has a terrible sense of God's condemnation. Like the rich man in the parable (Luke 12:16–21), Per Hansa has laid up treasures but he is "not rich toward God." His normative logic of good deeds and compensatory treasures elicits from Beret, grounded as she was in Luther's doctrine of *sola fide,* the somber pronouncement: "Woe unto you that are full!—For ye shall hunger. . . . Woe unto you that laugh now!—For ye shall weep and mourn" (431, Rölvaag's ellipsis). Referring to that other kingdom not of America, Beret adds in what was Rölvaag's own dark pessimism: "Not many from the Dakota prairie will ever stand in glory *there*" (432).

In faith she is an Abraham-figure leaving the others behind as she journeys toward her own Mount Moriah in search of that glory.

Before looking more closely at what can be called Beret's teleological suspension of the ethical, we should acknowledge the fact that Rölvaag places great importance upon the need for the immigrants to maintain rather than suspend their Norwegian culture in America. Was it not because the claims of a transcendent authority, in conflict with those of culture, demand a faith that many persons do not have; and, therefore, lest the immigrants forsake a religion too severe in its demands, Rölvaag sought to uphold a culture that regarded institutional religion as a necessary integrating force? He knew that a people without cultural roots become trivial in their values, expedient in their aims, and vulgar in their tastes. Furthermore, he knew that an individual in his singularity risks psychological breakdown if he abandons a sense of tradition. Most importantly, Rölvaag knew from his reading of Kierkegaard and Ibsen that religious claims are not always those of culture and that, as with the Sermon on the Mount, they may downright contradict them. The real dilemma Rölvaag sets before Per Hansa and Beret is not that of Norwegian versus American claims but that of culture per se on the one hand and an existential religious consciousness on the other. As between all or nothing, Per Hansa's cultural all becomes Beret's nothing, just as her religious all was his nothing.

Yet why does Rölvaag stress with such compulsion the need for the immigrants to retain their Norwegian traditions? Jorgenson and Solum provide abundant evidence that in his St. Olaf College lectures and his many speeches and sermons in the community Rölvaag argued for the continued nurture of these roots, especially those of language, the Lutheran church, and what he considered the personal traits of Scandinavians as a people. Perhaps reasons can be found in Rölvaag's deep loyalty to his own Norwegian roots, which he traumatically severed when he first came to America. The pain and guilt he suffered in leaving his parents shook him again and again. Nevertheless, despite his persistent call for cultural continuities, including institutional Lutheranism, this call has a penultimate emphasis at best, and the essential point finally has to do with religious claims. In spite of Beret's indomitable effort to preserve her Norwegian ways, her greater strivings concern a transcendent faith.

How to handle the religious level of experience in art has tortured many creative persons, including Kierkegaard, who lived to aver the ultimate discontinuity between art and religion, between imagination and faith.[33] Rölvaag never thought of himself as one to grapple with these theological subtleties, though from his early years he was interested in such speculation and, as a student at St. Olaf College, thought seriously of entering the ministry.[34] That he chose to be a teacher and novelist did not diminish this seriousness. When he came to write his second novel, *On Forgotten Paths* (1914), he was actuated partly by a desire to prove that religious experience could in fact be made the central element in a secular novel. And when he started *Giants in the Earth* in the autumn of 1923 his own religious consciousness had conceived of God as a being "who is searching and pressing and pushing even as life itself is."[35] Rölvaag's matrix, however, serves only to point in the direction of Beret's religious experience in the novel. This experience is best seen in the tension, already mentioned, between the Kierkegaardian levels exemplified by Per Hansa and herself. These ethical and religious levels serve to structure the novel, with Per Hansa dominating three-fourths of the narrative but giving way in the last portion to Beret. The pivot upon which the two parts rest is the unnamed Lutheran minister whose arrival at Spring Creek marks a striking change in the novel's tone, as the claims of one "kingdom" are now challenged by those of another.

Throughout the earlier part of the novel Per Hansa's vision and strength control the action with even more authority than do the forces of elemental nature. Beret's world is psychological, and her drama impinges upon the price she is paying for cultural uprootedness and Per Hansa's new kingdom. Psychological phenomena, however, fail to account for what happens to her with the minister's presence. Gradually her derangement subsides, new energy flows through her being, a certain peace not separate from strength comes to her, she moves with new "purpose and confidence" (409), whereas Per Hansa begins his irrevocable disintegration: "his face was deeply furrowed; his hair and beard, heavily sprinkled with grey, were now full of dust and straw" (409).

At first the minister performs certain ecclesiastical functions that the prairie folk had lived without since the founding of Spring Creek. Amusingly he reassures Syvert Tönseten, who was decidedly not ordained, that the marriage rites administered to Johannes Mörstad and his young wife, Josie, four years ago in the wilderness were legal. In his threadbare canonicals the minister holds communion; he preaches on the Israelites' coming into the Land of Canaan; he baptizes children, including Peder Victorious. Then the focus of his presence narrows upon Per Hansa and Beret and he sees woeful travail bordering on suicide for both. Alone with Per Hansa, the minister listens to the suffering man pour out his guilt for Beret's derangement and for the presumption in giving the "non-human" name of Victorious to his son Peder. Most importantly, as Per Hansa sits fearfully "ravaged and broken, like a forest maple shattered by a storm" (372), he confesses to a loss of purpose. Clutching the minister he asks, *What is the man to do?*" (373, Rölvaag's italics). What he hears in reply—"He shall humble himself before the Lord his God, and shall take up his cross to bear it with patience!" (373)— makes him burst out in bitter laughter, then desperately to ask again: "Did I do right or did I do wrong when I brought her out here?" (374). Supporting him in that fateful choice, the minister adds: "You are not willing to bear your cross with humility!" "No, I am not," Per Hansa answers, "and let me tell you something more. . . . We find other things to do out here than to carry crosses!" (374). Boasting of his deeds but not daring to confess his motives, Per Hansa trembles at the thought that his accomplishments were now being held under the light of divine judgment.

Yet he does not yield: he neither resigns himself to nor believes in an authority sovereign to his own. In his departure at the end of the novel to summon a minister and not a doctor for the dying Hans Olsa, his pride keeps him from seeing his mission as anything more than a perfunctory compliance with Beret's wishes. "Oh, well—here goes!" he says to himself, heading out into the frozen prairie for he knows not what (451).

His vision has been the big barn he will build the next fall— a real show barn, "red with white cornices." Beret's vision has been God's glory. The radical separateness between the two worlds has left Per Hansa bewildered, lost, his world "upside down" (443). Beret on the other hand has been stangely renewed. Admittedly Rölvaag was not at his artistic best when attempting to depict the mysterious workings of grace. Neither, one might say, were Tolstoy and Dostoevsky. The reader must be satisfied with intentionality; it seems clear that Rölvaag's aim was to account for Beret's transformation in other terms than those of psychology. What Rölvaag sought to do, as in *On Forgotten Paths*, was to make religious experience a decisive element in the novel. This effort required that he acknowledge the reality of efficacious Christian grace and its fruits of faith. It also meant he would struggle as an artist with the truths of sin and salvation, which have a way of disappearing into airy meaninglessness unless their existential correlatives have a local habitation.

No further caveats need interfere with an examination of what Rölvaag does when, for a second time, he brings the minister face to face with Beret. Early ministrations were the prelude for the sermon he now was to preach in the house of Per Hansa and Beret. The neighboring folk were seated tightly before him, and the trunk into which angst-ridden Beret had, as it were, descended now served as the holy altar. The topic he had chosen was that of God's glory—or rather the topic "had suggested itself powerfully to him on the day he had gone away after talking with Beret" (391). He had felt happy over his choice of the topic, but now in seeing her anguished condition his own faith suddenly faltered and his sermon became a "sorry mess" of disconnected phrases, terminated by "Come and behold the Glory of the Lord" (392,

395). Hollow as the words seemed at that moment to him, a power beyond his will had tongued them with divine meaning for Beret, such that "every day now since that remarkable man had placed his hand on her and in his prophetic voice had assured her that from this time forth she was released from the bonds of Satan" (400), a gracious healing was transfiguring her. With regenerate eyes she beheld her home filled with a new light, and she felt like someone who had been on a long journey (to Mount Moriah?) and returned again a partial stranger.

Jorgenson and Solum misread the novel at this point when they discount the religious element in Beret's experience and suggest that she is merely "temporarily relieved" through the influence of the minister.[36] Rölvaag's Lutheran heritage and his knowledge of Kierkegaard must have implanted within him a conviction as to the authenticity of religious experience. "Tired unto death," he once wrote about himself, "the wanderer has found that to which he may lean his head[:] In Jesus' holy bosom, / My soul shall rest / And drink of love's eternal fountain."[37] The same assurance describes the hymn Beret softly sings: "O sinner's friend, / Whom thorns did lend / Death's scornful coronation, / Grant me peace with God again, / And with it salvation" (430).

The authenticity given to Beret's religious experience comes in the way she resembles Kierkegaard's knight of faith who finds strength that is impotence, wisdom that is foolishness, hope that is madness, and love that is hatred of self. The knight of faith in Kierkegaard's *Fear and Trembling* discovers joy in the absurd and, like Abraham, believes "by virtue of the absurd."[38] The absurd is the paradox without which faith becomes only an extension of ethical choice. Kierkegaard rejected any concept of faith not based upon the radical distinction between religious faith and ethical choice. For Rölvaag's Beret the paradox of believing by virtue of the absurd meant that all motives and all achievements were challenged, including those of her husband and the whole immigrant community. In the challenge, moreover, was a singular and terrifying self-with-God relationship that required the particular to be higher than the universal and that left Beret separated from the rest, face to face with her destiny, with God himself who had singled her out. Something of this mystery comes to the dying Hans Olsa when he says, "It is terrible to fall into the hands of the living God" (438). It is the realization that death brings a person face to face with the God against whom he has sinned, who makes demands upon him that he cannot fulfill, and yet without whom he cannot live. It is the moment, as Rölvaag wrote in his opening sentence of *Boat of Longing* (1921), when "utmost Light and utmost Dark hold tryst." Kierkegaard calls this an "existential pathos."[39] Beret and, in his final moments, Hans Olsa know it experientially. By contrast Per Hansa, in his confused but adamant self-willfulness, can only call his friend's religious faith "blasphemy" (438).

The distinctions between faith and choice, religion and ethics, the particular and the universal, becoming and doing, subjectivity and cultural norms serve to explain the separate worlds of Beret and Per Hansa. These distinctions suggest the further Kierkegaardian theme of "offensiveness" that Rölvaag assimilated. From the regulative view of Per Hansa's world, the divine imperatives Beret obeys are an outrage and affront. They are an offense. In Per Hansa's totally human scheme Hans Olsa's avowal is even blasphemous. At issue is the ground of being itself. When the authority of God-fearingness collides with that of human initiative, hard work, fortitude, and imagination; when God's order contradicts human expectations; when, in Kierkegaard's terms, the particular contravenes the universal, or when a transcendent kingdom challenges the new American one, the result is an offense to those persons committed in each case to the latter and to those whose foundations of self-reliance have been truly shaken. In nineteenth-century America a system of prudential ethics found offense in the religious inwardness that characterized Lutheranism at its core. It is instructive to read Kierkegaard's *Training in Christianity*, especially part 2, entitled "The Offense,"[40] in light of the collision that occurs between Beret and Per Hansa—a collision that had its American origins as far back as the seventeenth-century controversy between Calvinist piety on the one hand and the whole Arminian spirit of moralism on the other. Kierkegaard dared his nineteenth-century readers, themselves influenced by the same compromising moralism, to confront the meaning of Christ's words, "Blessed is he, whosoever shall not be offended in me" (Matt. 11:6; Luke 7:23). When the worlds of Christ and culture collide, the possibility of the offense is not to be avoided: "thou must pass through it," Kierkegaard wrote, "and thou canst be saved from it one way only—by believing."[41]

For Christ's listeners, who wanted bread to satisfy their hunger, it was outrageous to be told, "I am the bread of life" (John 6:35). "Doth this offend you?" he asked (6:61). Their assumptions had determined their expectations. Christ's was a different logic—a chronometrical or absolute kind of logic, as Melville called it in *Pierre*—whereas the people followed a horological kind, practical and relative. Again, the clash is the offense. To Kierkegaard the possibility of offense is present every instant.[42] *Giants in the Earth* ends at such a moment. Beret's celestial vision condemns the terrestrial one of her husband. "You know what our life has been: land and houses, and then more land, and cattle. . . . Can't you understand that a human being ever becomes concerned over his sins and wants to be freed from them?" To her indictment Per Hansa answers, "I suppose I don't understand anything, do I?" (442). Bewildered by a religious faith that turns his practical world "upside down" and that could "twist things around in a queer way" (443), he falls back on his own assumptions and expectations. In reviewing them he muses: "All his life he had worked and slaved in order that she and the children might be made comfortable . . . and now it was flung in his face and he was taunted with being only a blind mole who saw nothing but the hole he had burrowed himself into!" (443–44, Rölvaag's ellipsis).

That Per Hansa yields to Beret at the cost of his life does not point to the direction future Americans would take. Rölvaag's next two novels make this point emphatic enough. Americans would tolerate no such taunting and accept no such condemnation. Their kingdom would need no reliance upon divine initiative, and it would harbor no concern for any so-called offense. Yet we have Beret's judgment and her vision.

This is not to say that Rölvaag stands unequivocally with Beret. He admired Per Hansa's barn-building; indeed he transformed this immigrant Norwegian into a pioneer giant whose heroic will enabled him to bear any load. Yet for all his strength, Per Hansa refuses the one burden the minister calls him to take up. No, says the giant of the earth, "We find other things to do out here than to carry crosses!" (374). Rölvaag has struck here his profoundest level of irony, its antithesis reflected in Beret's strength of spirit.

That Rölvaag stands closer to Beret than to Per Hansa remains intriguing speculation. Perhaps the more cautious estimate is that he stands closer to Beret than has been generally assumed. What seems clear, however, is that Kierkegaard's ideas never stopped simmering, and that the distinction he drew between the tragic hero who exists on the ethical level and the knight of faith who exists on the religious level informed Rölvaag's major writing. To Rölvaag the demands of great art exceeded even the question of all or nothing; to him art demanded nothing less than the impossible.[43] A clue to what Rölvaag meant comes in his analysis of Ibsen's *Peer Gynt,* first on the level of aesthetics, then on that of ethics, and finally on that of religion. It is on this level, he said, that Ibsen's play "glorifies the efficacy of unselfish sacrifice. We might state the ideal thus: 'Take up your cross and follow me!' "[44] Per Hansa might be a great American, but Beret is a truer Christian. And Rölvaag knew the difference.

He spoke through Beret a warning not only to the characters with whom she was in conflict but quite directly to his readers. Unfortunately, most readers simply write her off as a madwoman, but she is also a voice in what Rölvaag saw as the growing whirlwind of American materialism. He also used the stark contrast between her and Per Hansa in their frontier setting to show the same deep conflict between American ways and European ways that one finds in Henry James and

with less power and imagination in Willa Cather. But Rölvaag's deeper intention was to reveal the struggles of the spirit
through a profoundly troubled pair of central characters,
clashing not about manners and mores but about salvation
and damnation. At the same time, he was too much the novelist and too little the apologist to portray Beret all glowing in
white and Per Hansa in darkness. She too is possessed and
obsessed, and one cannot see her as totally embodying
goodness and truth; her destructiveness, her eagerness for
punishment, her pessimism, and her horror of the slighest
deviation from tradition cannot be taken as a portrayal of a
character whose religious impulses have brought her to the
celestial city. Rölvaag did not create a visible saint in Beret,
and he knew his Lutheran orthodoxy too well to suppose that
regeneration transfigures a human being in this world. As
Luther wrote, original sin, after regeneration, is like a wound
that, though it is in the course of healing, "still runs and is
sore."[45]

IV

Although Rölvaag never broke prairie sod, he knew the
immigrant experience firsthand. He knew what it was to leave
home, family, and fatherland, and to make his way in a
strange, new culture. Throughout his adult life he brooded
over the cost of immigration, not just in lives but in souls, and
he made it the central theme in his fiction. The theme touched
the core of Rölvaag's own complex interior and darkened it
with tragic shadowings. To lose a fatherland without finding
another left him a stranger, separated from those who stayed
behind and those in his midst. To live in two worlds but
belong to neither was the cost Rölvaag, like Beret, paid. Saying this does not discount other facets of Rölvaag's personality. Indeed, he bore the image of Per Hansa as well as that of
Peder Victorious, the one possessing what Jorgenson and
Solum call a "viking heart" and the other a "penetrating skeptical intelligence."[46] But something in his makeup ran more

deeply, something stemming perhaps from the tragic drowning of his young son, Paul Gunnar, in 1920, the same year he started to write *Boat of Longing*, soon to be followed by *Giants in the Earth*. Whatever the origin, something made him ever more conscious of the tragedy associated with life itself. For him the immigrant came to personify the alienation common to everyone, a human condition in which one lives in many worlds but belongs nowhere, the fate of existence presaging what this century's history has corroborated in its millions of displaced, deracinated people worldwide, belonging nowhere and blown about willy-nilly. Rölvaag's viking heart and skeptical intelligence had deeper levels. In identifying them Jorgenson and Solum note how "Beret is the deep undercurrent of dread, agony, sorrow, anxiety that ran through his life like a dark October stream."[47] Rölvaag knew firsthand the immigrant experience of dread and alienation. Like Beret's inner world, his was a labyrinth of solitude in which he wandered often as a stranger. Beret was his anima—his setting out, his headland edge of darkness, his lostness—as remembered in his broken ties from Norway and a loving mother left behind.

Even while recuperating in Biloxi, Mississippi, in 1929, Rölvaag accepted the fact that his angina pectoris soon would mean his death. Seeing how the ocean waves came washing in to be destroyed on the beach, he wrote to his friend Lincoln Colcord: "Not one turns back to tell the others. Not one takes thought of what happens to the one in the lead." He continued: "Natures like yours and mine can never be happy! It isn't possible. We live too deeply. . . ."[48] Nothing stays the inexorable ways of destiny, certainly not one's ancestral roots. Yet how tragic to sever these roots before one's time, and to think the American prize a compensation.

This was his lament, but the cultural and psychological consequences of immigration carried profoundly religious meaning too, making immigration for Rölvaag a tragic adventure akin to religious angst. Translated as "dread," the term identifies the fundamental affective state of human existence, and discloses the perilous position between freedom and possibility, between what a person is and what he is obliged to become.

To live within this tension is more than most people can bear. Yet somehow Beret bore it but not without the price of brokenness. "I saw," Rölvaag wrote, "that the woman must go mad from suffering."[49] She had given up her homeland and all its inexpressible associations that nurtured selfhood on many levels. Descending into the soul's dark night, its angst, was Beret's solitary journey. Her dark trunk was her final refuge. How her death becomes a rebirth and the trunk an altar is the story of healing that Rölvaag said he had not thought to write before beginning to study the influence of the church in the early pioneer community.[50]

A haunting similarity strikes one who recalls Hawthorne's Dimmesdale, the analogy between his heartfelt agony and Beret's, his dark night and hers. One also notes analogy between Hester's unrepentant self and Per Hansa's, both characters more representative of America's ideological promise than are their tormented counterparts. The fact is not lost upon the modern reader who still prefers visible heroism to the other, darker, inner kind.

4
John Muir's West: Romantic
Apotheosis and Calvinist Shadowings

I

The West that Ole Rölvaag's Per Hansa faced was the West of infinite possibility. That he was still facing it in death suggests either the irony of the Western myth or the unfulfilled promise of it. To settle upon the irony is to see that Per Hansa, along with the other conquering Western heroes, conquered nothing in spite of his achievements vis-à-vis nature. Death, the ultimate law of nature, is the only conqueror. If, however, there is still more of the Western myth to know and more of its promise to realize, then one may entertain a bigger Romanticism and look elsewhere than to Rölvaag for its apotheosis. A well-worn signpost pointing to this further frontier is Thoreau's essay, "Walking" (1862), in which he equates the West with the wild, proclaiming that "in Wildness is the preservation of the World." He means as well the preservation of the human spirit. To be in touch with the strength and marrow of nature, which is what Thoreau means by the wild, is to live in the realm of the holy, a *sanctum sanctorum*. The response to this new existence is not to be a conqueror of nature but to become a kindred spirit with it by purging oneself of all that is not nature. In such kinship lies the heart of primitivism and the return to one's origins in the sacred.

The place of this apotheosis was supposedly the West,

somewhere out on the frontier beyond civilization. In this
enlarged Romanticism, uniting the human spirit with nature's
essence, the frontier signified something more than one of its
famous interpreters, Frederick Jackson Turner, understood.
We shall see that a far more profound interpreter, who sought
the spectrum of experiential validation, was the immigrant
John Muir. As for Turner, he failed to push his frontier thesis
far enough. He stopped at the point where the frontiersman
donned buckskin moccasins and took scalps in "orthodox
Indian fashion."[1] But about the reaches of primitivism Turner
did not speculate. The frontier, he said, was a safety valve for
the civilized albeit restless American, but Turner never really
said what the safety value opened unto. Ignorant about this
deeper wildness, he was satisfied to say in theoretical terms
that the frontier allowed a brief exposure to primitivism, a
sampling of it, as if this return to ancestral wellsprings would
provide the psychic charge needed to thrust the evolutionary
process higher. He saw the frontier as a microcosm where
human history from primitivism to civilization was
reenacted. The inviolable process from the one to the other
always spelled progress which, in turn, implied the frontiersman's expanded consciousness of his true mercantile errand
and martial obligations. But Turner the researcher, scholar,
teacher, and lecturer knew little about the frontier experience
itself except what he learned from maps, statistics, and historical documents. Ray Allen Billington insists that Turner had a
"love affair with the wilderness," but an affair usually lacks
commitment and abandonment. Turner's was nurtured by
summer vacations in Maine and California, and blighted most
of the time by guilt because he was not getting his writing
done. Concerning the "native races" (the Indians), Turner
paid scant attention. He saw them, Billington says, "only as
retarding the advance of civilization and 'compelling society
to organize and consolidate in order to hold the frontier.'"[2]

Turner went on to say in 1893 that the frontier was closed,
but he missed the irony. To him and his frontiersmen, including the sequence of frontier types—trappers, cattlemen, min-
ers, pioneer farmers, equipped farmers, town dwellers, city

industrialists—the frontier had never been open, not in the full meaning of primitivism. Neither had it been open to the Parkmans, the Irvings, and the Twains who journeyed out to have a look at it. For Turner the frontier, signifying a dividing line between civilization and savagery, could be described with demographic statistics; for the others it was little more than an anthropological museum of Indian customs, or a setting of wonder for heroic adventurers, or a land of tobacco-chewing prospectors. The point has to do with other significances than those Turner found, and with other experiences than those conquest, exploitation, or curiosity offer up. Lacking an understanding of primitivism and its myths, Turner merely presupposed man standing in conflict with nature and having final dominion to transform what he could not assimilate. Rebirth meant to be reenergized and rechallenged to dominate nature, to manipulate and utilize it. In the end the true frontiersmen were John D. Rockefeller, Marcus Hanna, Andrew Carnegie, and all other captains of American industry whose achievement over nature proved the self to be the supreme creative force.

By contrast, the primitivism Thoreau made integral with the West fused God, man, and nature into one cosmic unity in which all distinctions disappear. One recent interpreter, William Everson, believes this pantheistic primitivism is "not only the basic Californian or Western point of view, but is essentially American, is indeed *the* characteristic American religious and aesthetic feeling."[3] Here we have still another perspective of the true American character. The argument concerns pantheism as the root force, the primal and authentic impulse in the American consciousness. Pantheism dispels the separateness of God, man, and nature; it combines all into the All, the cosmos. According to Everson, its microcosm is the West—the West as archetype, as *the* essential American experience, as true primitivism.

Something needs to be said about this larger view personified by the Westerner who, even though never hearing of pantheism and caring nothing about it if he had, nevertheless lived amid the mysteries of the land, sensing in unconscious but collective ways his psychic relationship to it. The reference here is not to Turner's frontiersman whose contact with primitivism served to quicken his self-affirmation and strengthen his resolve to take the land. It is instead to the mountain man, portrayed by such writers as Vardis Fisher, A. B. Guthrie, Jr., and Don Berry, and studied by historians, moviemakers, and literary critics alike. As depicted, the mountain man of the Rockies donned buckskins and took his share of human scalps. He subsisted on what he received from furs that he trapped. However, he lived within the deeper rhythms of nature as the original inhabitants, the Indians, had done for ages before his arrival. His concern was less to control nature than to be alert to it for his next meal and higher truths. The mountain man was different from the pioneers who followed after him because he could hear in nature what others could not and see what others found invisible. Delinquent in matters of societal laws, he was keenly attuned to nature's laws not only for his survival but for a sense of belonging. Admittedly a certain mythical aura surrounds this interpretation. Bernard DeVoto, Henry Nash Smith, and Billington have interpreted the mountain man differently: as daring but degraded, fleeing to the frontier because he was unable or unwilling to conform to social restriction. Others have interpreted him as the expectant capitalist: ambitious, hard-driving, acquisitive, eager to gain wealth. This pragmatic view, however, fails to capture the whole truth about him.[4] The mountain man *was* a different breed, and the difference lies in the fact that he lived in a world that had not yet been demythologized. He sensed the Indians' consciousness of a totally alive, pantheistic world, and to some degree wanted to make it his own. He was no more interested in Christianizing or civilizing the Indians than he was in imposing his will upon nature. The mountain man was the Westerner who sought the ultimate merger with the ways of nature and the ways of the Indians whose shamanistic culture made nature sacred and whose *tamanawas* experience made them one with this sacredness.

Again the effort was to know experientially another dimension, to cross this more distant frontier, even to touch the "original" truth, though being wary of ever claiming possession of it. One way was to marry Indian women. Another was to assimilate Indian dress, crafts, art. The most audacious way was to have a *tamanawas* experience—that is, to go into the forest or the mountains, to fast, to hallucinate if necessary, in order that in a visionary moment some natural object might take on individual sacramental meaning and thus serve as a link between the one world and the other. The *tamanawas* became the transfigured object—a bird, a tree, a river—or the religious experience eventuating in the transformation. It was in this experience that the white man merged with nature and became one with its aboriginal inhabitants. Racial distinctions were dissolved. So also were distinctions between nature and God. The cost to the initiate was nothing less than everything, including his ego. But the reward was the certainty, as Don Berry says in his remarkable novel *Trask* (1960), that "this tree wishes you no harm. . . . Go around it in peace."[5] To exist in conflict with the tree is to war against oneself and the universe. By contrast, primitivism affirms a world of original relationships in which human beings realize their full potentiality only as they participate in this archaic level of reality. Wholeness of being is a matter of total relationship—not dependency, certainly not separateness, and least of all conquest.

Before we consider John Muir as one who sought to personify the larger Romanticism and believed he could interpret the West accordingly, it is worthwhile to follow Everson's argument further. With stunning audacity he traces the ramifications of primitivism, holding it as the clue for an understanding of the West. He wants nothing to do with the old God-man relationship of sovereignty and dependency. He finds no meaning in Puritan John Winthrop's famous definition of true liberty as restricted liberty. Hierarchical structure is anathema and non-Western. Everson eschews the tragic implications of the self that wars against God, moral restraints, and nature. He rejects any assumption that identifies human existence with polarities, encounters, struggles. His archetype is a pantheistic West empty of hierarchy, polarity, fallenness, and ambiguity, but totally "suffused by the presence of the Other."[6]

To speak of a Western apotheosis recalls Melville's panegyric: "Take heart, take heart, O Bulkington! Bear thee grimly, demigod! Up from the spray of thy ocean-perishing—straight up leaps thy apotheosis" (*Moby-Dick*, chap. 23). As in Brueghel's painting of Icarus plunging into the sea, the uprising spray takes the momentary shape of a crown symbolizing the tragic but kingly self still inviolable even in the death-maw of the sea. Everson's Western apotheosis is not tragic, and assuredly is not reenacted in Brueghel's scene. In the contrast no tragic irony beclouds what Everson calls the "privacy of discovery," nor does it obscure the relationship between "the gods of the solar system [and] the gods of the solar plexus."[7] The "Westward-hungering consciousness" is for him a synthesis of region and being, each serving the other in glorious wholeness. "Western" comes to be synonymous with mystical, primal, archaic, religious, cosmic.

Although in some respects Everson's theory is warmed-over Whitman and Thoreau, exotic Big Sur stuff, it carries a stridently provocative argument for the Western archetype with the artist as its embodiment. Not the mountain man, not the pioneer, but the Western artist is the real frontiersman. Attesting to this distinction is his "scale of imagination, the repudiation of received forms, the eruptive intensity of the energy, the monumental output, the aloof, transcendental passion, the overwhelming pantheistic vision."[8] According to Everson, the voice best giving utterance to these grand qualities was that of Robinson Jeffers; Joaquin Miller was the archetype's inceptor and Edwin Markham its amplifier, but Jeffers was its embodied apotheosis. Close to Jeffers for sheer Dionysiac energy was Frank Norris whose *The Octopus* Everson calls the West's *Moby-Dick* and whose portrayal of the artist Presley captured the immensity of the Western imagination and mythical consciousness. Not until the writings of Kenneth Rexroth, Jack Kerouac, Lawrence Ferlinghetti, and Gary Snyder did the archetype once again have its "constellated" voices.

The frontiersman today, then, is the artist to whom the mantle of primitive consciousness has been passed, enabling him to achieve the apotheosis that awakens modern man from his spiritual somnolence. This is Everson's faith. Little matter that that consciousness feels a penchant for violence one moment, a disquieting lassitude the next, and frequently a preoccupation with death; that California's official flower is the poppy; or that the whole Western archetype has a dark strain, a death-pulse, which writers like Jack London and George Sterling knew well. The theme of Everson's argument is that certain Western artists have penetrated into the wildness, there to discover the true frontier to be a passage leading to fuller existence best described as primitive, pantheistic apotheosis. Those who achieve this existence are able to identify the myth of the West with salvation, including their own.

Although not new, this thesis establishes primitivism as central in the American character despite three centuries of alien ideologies to expunge it. Unfortunately, Everson fails to resolve the nagging problem that, like one's hearing a fly buzz at the moment of transcendence, even the most rapturous vision emanating from primitive consciousness never succeeds in expunging America's other inheritances, including the dark shadow emanating from Jerusalem and slicing through the Western archetype. The truth may be one of irreconcilable opposites. Even in its farthest primitivist reaches American Romanticism still failed to cancel a colliding Christian consciousness.

The tension makes the Scottish immigrant John Muir an arresting study. Popular estimates interpret him as a supreme mountain man in his own right who succeeded in influencing governmental policies to preserve much of the West's wilderness. His writings call attention to a fine lyrical kinship with nature that distinguishes Muir as a great American Romantic, perhaps the last to commit both mind and heart to know the West and then to write it as well as live it. Yet deep

within his inner landscape were the vestiges of a religious
orthodoxy that he could not and, in the end, sought not to
expunge.

II

To what extent the tension between Romanticism and an
inherited Calvinism influenced John Muir becomes an important issue in any assessment of his life and writing. It is true
that on the surface he appears to have exchanged his father's
Calvinist teachings for the Romanticism of nineteenth-
century America. Evidence comes directly from his own
autobiography, *The Story of My Boyhood and Youth*, written
in 1908 after he had become famous. But Thomas J. Lyon
raises the intriguing possibility that perhaps Muir's public
persona required a simpler story, or even that Muir had genu-
inely forgotten the intellectual struggles and contradictions of
his early years. The important question Professor Lyon asks
is how "the ideas in Muir's authoritarian upbringing could
have been so completely reversed in his mature philosophy."
For, Lyon argues, "there is not a single point in the theory of
Calvinism which Muir, the man, failed to overthrow."
Roderick Nash is persuaded that one of "several formidable
obstacles" Muir overcame was "a father whose Calvinistic
conception of Christianity brooked no religion of nature."
Similarly, Kevin Starr thinks that Muir's conversion to a religious reverence for nature "filled the void left by an abandoned Calvinism and cured some of its scars."[9]

It is, I think, too easy to say that Muir abandoned Calvinism. What is more important to recognize is how his early
training deepened his religious perspectives and sharpened the
conflicts within himself that Romanticism could never annul.
At the age of seventy-four he wrote with admiration that his
father had been like the New England Puritans—"types of the
best American pioneers whose unwavering faith in God's
eternal righteousness forms the basis of our country's
greatness." Despite his father's stern piety, John Muir did not
develop an antagonism to religious orthodoxy. William Fred-

eric Badè insists that Muir's father "had no such effect upon John." Nor, according to Badè, did Muir relax his hold on the "essentials" of his Protestant faith, despite the fact that his sympathies leaned towards religious liberalism. In breaking away from his father's narrow Biblicism, he adopted a more rational historical interpretation of the Bible that saved his faith in both religion and science. "The two books [nature and the Bible]," Muir said, "harmonize beautifully, and contain enough of divine truth for the study of all eternity." Yet even this affirmation fails to hide an anxious preoccupation over the great doctrines of the fall of man and the wonders of redeeming love about which, Muir confessed, nature is silent: "It is so much easier for us to employ our faculties upon these beautifully tangible forms than to exercise a simple, humble living faith."[10]

Most people know John Muir as a keen observer of nature and a wide-ranging traveler who, by the end of the century, had become a powerful voice in influencing legislation regarding national parks and forests. But to understand the deeper John Muir it is necessary to see that behind these activities was a mind at work trying to reconcile conflicting ideas that pertained, on the one hand, to nature that conforms to the mind's eye and projects the drama of one's developing self; and, on the other hand, to nature as divine emanation, as revelation, as typological figure presupposing a distinctly separate and sovereign God. With the first, religious experience celebrates the self as reconciler of all things visible and invisible and the word as symbol of this reconciliation. With the second, the experience sharpens the distinction between the self and the greater infinitude of spirit, and makes praising God an acknowledgment of one's own dependency. For Muir, the dilemma between a Romantic and a Calvinist sense of self had its roots in his studies at the University of Wisconsin and, before that, in his Scottish family's heritage.

At the University he had encountered Darwinian evolution, including studies in botany and glaciation. Even more importantly, he had read the Concord philosophers and the English Romantic poets. Coincidentally, Professor Ezra S.

Carr, who taught Muir the theory of Ice Age glaciation, was a personal friend of Emerson, and Muir's classics professor, James D. Butler, was a thoroughgoing Emersonian. It was at this time that Muir began to take seriously what Wordsworth (whom he quoted often) called the "sense sublime of something far more deeply interfused." I think it correct to call Muir a Romantic, perhaps the last important one of our nineteenth-century national literature. As such, he was committed to discover nature's transcendent meaning that he believed informed himself as well. Perhaps it is an irony worth noting that even though Muir's sight in one eye was impaired from an accident in 1867, he emphatically did not have the singleness of Newton's vision that the Romantics decried. Muir's was a transcendental eye that perceived all things material and spiritual in relationship and himself harmonious with all things. Literally hundreds of passages from his books and journals document his search for that sublimity known to the Romantic consciousness as natural supernaturalism. In reading Muir one is constantly made aware that nature to him was emblematic and, moreover, that he would find in nature corroboration of his own selfhood and its salvation.

But in sharp conflict with Romanticism and its underlying ideas was the Calvinism instilled into young Muir by his father and the Scottish practice of orthodox piety. Muir recalled with emphasis that his father required daily Bible study. By the time the boy was eleven he had learned large sections of the Old and New Testament "by heart and by sore flesh." For Daniel Muir, the father, there was no question about the doctrines of salvation only through Christ's atonement and eternal punishment for the unregenerate. For the young son the severity of these doctrines was reinforced by the menacing North Sea storms, the chill ruins of the old Dunbar castle nearby, and the father's obsessive example of hard work that the rest of the family was expected to follow. As immigrants later clearing land in Wisconsin, the father on occasions would say to his son John tending huge brush fires: "Now John, just think what an awful thing it would be to be thrown into that fire:—and then think of hell-fire, that is so many times hotter." The stern Calvinist and biblical literalist never relented, looking with suspicion upon his son's later scientific studies and regarding his singular passion for exploring nature as sinful. "You are God's property," he warned, "soul and body and substance—give those powers up to their owner!"[11]

Even though Muir's decision to know mountains, not unlike Thoreau's to know beans, was an act of courage, he remained uneasy in not taking his father's dogma straight, and troubled that his conversion to a religion of nature might itself become his literary subject. Again the problem was self. He wanted his subject to be the glorious and interfusing light of nature—the sovereign light that transfigures nature when beheld by the eye that itself had been transfigured by divine grace. In relation to his subject his words would be nothing more than incidental, his role as a writer radically subordinated. But Romanticism heralded the ego, the expanding consciousness, the union of self and light. It also proclaimed, in Emersonian terms, that the artist's words would be God's wine. It was this Romantic faith in the infinitude of self that Calvinism challenged, admonishing that unless the self acknowledges its limits and redirects its celebration towards the wholly otherness of God, the human being stands perilously close to destruction as he declares his sovereignty.

Before we examine what this dilemma meant for Muir, the writer, it is instructive to trace Muir's grand commitment to Romanticism. For he was determined to know the Sierras as *his* "Range of Light" and to experience union with this light. Seeing the Cumberland Mountains on his 1867 walking trip to Florida, recorded in his journal that was published in 1917 as *A Thousand-Mile Walk to the Gulf,* he hinted at what he would feel when seeing the Sierras for the first time. The Cumberlands, he wrote, were "the first real mountains that my foot ever touched or eyes beheld"; and his first mountain stream, the Emory River, seemed, he said, "to feel the presence of the great Creator." But nothing in this book is more prophetic than his description, on the final page, of his first seeing the Sierras. He had sailed from Florida to Cuba, then to New York, then to San Francisco, and three days later had set out for the mountains. When still fifty or more miles away he felt their "spiritual power." You "bathe in these spirit-beams," he wrote, and presently "you lose consciousness of your separate existence: you blend with the landscape, and become part and parcel of nature."[12]

Taken from Emerson's *Nature*, this description indicates Muir's awareness that paralleling his studies of glacial phenomena was an exciting conversion taking place within himself. About this event the public knew little until 1911 (Muir was seventy-three) when he published a handful of old journal notes under the title *My First Summer in the Sierra*. To call this a "spiritual autobiography," as one critic does,[13] suggests something of the overwhelming thrill, the sense of joy and wonder that permeates this most remarkable book. In its journal form beginning with 3 June 1869, the book records nothing less than Muir's spiritual awakening as well as his incomparably vivid accounts of the Yosemite Valley. Up the Merced River and into the Valley itself, which to Muir was like an Edenic garden, he beheld sights that left him too ex-cited to sleep: thundering falls, streams, precipices three thousand feet high fringed with trees—"everything kept in joyful rhythmic motion in the pulses of Nature's big heart." Matching the grandeur was the mystery of every hidden cell of a tree, every fibre of leaf and root, "throbbing with music and life." One glorious Sierra day followed another, dissolv-ing and absorbing and sending him "pulsing onward" into what he called true freedom, "a good practical sort of immor-tality." Stones were "altars," Yosemite Valley a "temple," and he a "pilgrim" amid the "holy mountains." Images of communion, baptism, and resurrection tell what was happen-ing to him. He announced his ascent of Cathedral Peak, for example, to be "the first time I have been at church in Califor-nia." Being baptized three times in one day—first in "balmy sunshine," then in "mysterious rays of beauty" emanating from the plant corolla, then in "the spray of the lower Yose-mite Falls": by immersion, by pouring, by sprinkling—should convince all Baptists, he wrote to his brother David, "that I've 'got religion.' " He had crossed the "Range of Light" where now, he said, he would like to dwell forever. "Here with bread and water I should be content . . . the morning stars still singing together and all the sons of God shouting for joy."[14]

That for over forty years Muir repressed his journal describing this remarkable summer suggests that the journal indeed records the unrepressed theme of the awakened self, the transformed ego, and serves as a Romantic testament. The dilemma ever haunting Muir was to abnegate the self, yet to rejoice in its fullness; to write about objective nature, yet to have his words experientially rooted in nature. When he set off in the autumn of 1874, after a ten-month hiatus in Oakland, he headed toward Mount Shasta, this time even more determined to experience the harmony between his soul and the impulses of nature, and to entice others to do the same. "Heaven knows that John the Baptist was not more eager to get all his fellow sinners into the Jordan than I to baptize all of mine in the beauty of God's mountains," he wrote. Walking wearily alone over the braided folds of the Sacramento Valley, he caught sight of the mountain while he was still a long way off. At that moment, he remembered later, "all my blood turned to wine, and I have not been weary since."[15]

Muir was determined to discover his real identity in the American West, including its mountains and forests. It was a Romantic identity he sought, one that was part and parcel of nature, one that in its primitivism became sacramental by his taking what he called "Sequoia wine, Sequoia blood." Others tried to call him back. After reading the account of his storm-swept night on Mount Shasta, his aging father pleaded, "You cannot warm the heart of the saint of God with your cold icy-topped mountains. O, my dear son, come away from them to the spirit of God and His holy word." Emerson, whom he had met in the Yosemite in 1871, urged him to leave his wild mountains and to become a teacher in some Eastern college. Still others who saw this tall immigrant Scotsman with unkempt beard and tattered clothes emerging from the mountains only rarely to supply himself with bread and tea tried to persuade him to stay down, even arguing, as did his Wisconsin friend, Emily Pelton, that he was sacrificing the "refining influence" of society. His resolve remained steadfast. To all who would beckon him downward his reply was the same: "I will not be done here for years. I am in no hurry. . . . I will fuse in spirit skies." His words testify to the unmistakable theme: the paradise to be achieved by the fulfillment of self in union with nature and its transcendent order.[16]

Muir was, he said, "hopelessly and forever a mountaineer."[17] He was also hopelessly and forever a Romantic, driven by the need to assimilate everything into himself and then to write of his own expanding consciousness—to make this his real theme. Muir's problem was not merely the dilemma of scientific objectivity on the one hand and subjective feeling on the other. The deeper problem was what to do with the self. Emerson, for whom Muir cherished a near-worshipful admiration, had said in *Nature:* "I am nothing; I see all." The pronouncement seemed to call for an annihilation of self as the prerequisite for cosmic vision. The real meaning, however, had nothing to do with the transformation that religious orthodoxy described as the corruptible exchanged for the incorruptible through Christ's atonement; rather, it heralded a Romantic enlargement of self, an awakened self that intuits all things as part and parcel of one's own identity. Romantic consciousness is not one of self-abnegation *(crucis)* nor is it a total absorption into the divine glory concealed behind the images and shadows of nature. On the contrary, the "I" remains sovereign; the currents of the godhead, said Emerson, "circulate through me." The great Romantic theme is that of self, as enunciated in Whitman's credo from *Leaves of Grass:* "I celebrate myself . . . I dote on myself."

What this means for the writer, as Romantic, is a powerful assertion of self-consciousness. For all his primitive mysticism, the Romantic artist must assert a consciousness of supreme selfhood and transform this heightened sense into artistic vision. He sees all and becomes all through a shaping imagination, a creativity, that preserves, stabilizes, and imbues with significance his experience, and in the end he makes the creation—his own word—ultimate and absolute. Muir would have the spiritual; he was not sure he wanted the literary.

Even though Muir was a prolific writer, he was reluctant to take up serious "book-making," waiting until he was nearly sixty to publish his first book, *The Mountains of California*, in 1894. The truth seems to be that writing for publication filled him with frustration and despair. "No amount of word-making," he said, "will ever make a single soul to *know* these mountains." He insisted that language held no compelling fascination; words, he said, are only "made of mud, for muddy purposes." This deprecation grew from a deep suspicion that going public with words required a certain hypocrisy. "Book-making," he wrote to Mrs. Jeanne C. Carr in 1872, "frightens me, because it demands so much artificialness and retrograding." Something struck him as "not quite honorable" in transforming "raw bush sugar and mountain meal into magazine cookies and snaps."[18]

I am not suggesting that in publishing his earlier scientific writings in the *Overland Monthly* during the early 1870s Muir wrestled with the problem of his identity as a writer. He was, after all, a scientist intent upon proving the glacial origins of the Yosemite and in refuting the theory of cataclysmic origins held by Professor Josiah D. Whitney of Harvard, the official state geologist of California, whose *The Yosemite Guide-Book* was a standard work of the time. Yet Muir, the writer, was anxious about who he really was. Indefatigable as a naturalist and wonderfully exuberant as a traveler, he grew sorely uneasy with the fact that writing demands an assertive ego that first assimilates the world and then imparts it again as an extension of the consciousness that first transformed it. Muir realized to his fear that transforming the world through consciousness and then fixing it into language meant a celebration of ego as the transforming instrument, and it was here that Muir quavered at the possibility, tempting to be sure, that to sing of the world would be to sing of himself.

Unaware of the opposite effect their psychology had,

friends urged Muir to write autobiography, assuring him that his books would be "Literature!" To Richard Watson Gilder's promptings in 1898 Muir answered, "My life on the whole has been level and uneventful. . . . I am not anxious to tell what I have done, but what Nature has done—an infinitely more important story." This, after years of thrilling exploration! To Walter Hines Page, who also urged Muir to write about himself, he answered in a similar vein: "My life has been so smooth and regular and reasonable, so free from blundering exciting adventures, the story seems hardly worth while in the midst of so much that is infinitely more important." Celebrating his personal journeys looked "too much like having to say, 'Here is the Lord, and here is Me!' "[19] It was the latter subject that Muir eschewed in his public writing. In his private letters and journals it was often the only subject.

In a sense the force of Muir's personality made everything he wrote autobiographical. His resoluteness to get as near the heart of things as he could, and to know it as his own, filled his writings with joyful discovery. Books like *The Mountains of California* (1894), *Our National Parks* (1901), and *The Yosemite* (1912), all published during his lifetime, not only describe the then still unspoiled garden of the American West but reveal Muir's reverence for life, for its spirit and secrets. However, his letters and journals, most of them published after he died in 1914, touch the deeper currents of self, many of them shaped according to the Christian myth of the fall, the redemption, and the emergence of a restored paradise.

III

To examine this level of Muir the writer, whose consciousness spanned both the Romantic and the Calvinist worlds, it is helpful once again to look at what his so-called Romantic conversion might have meant and, again, to trace his concomitantly symbolic travels. As for his conversion, M. H. Abrams has explained that a conspicuous Romantic tendency was to reconstitute "the stark drama and suprarational mysteries of the Christian story and doctrines" in such a way as to save the "experiential" relevance of the doctrines while making them "intellectually acceptable" to a post-Enlightenment age. What this meant for Wordsworth, who serves as Abrams's Romantic prototype, was a shift from the orthodox view of heaven, Jehovah, and hell to the world within—to the mind of man in the act of finding within itself what will suffice. Accordingly, Romanticism became a "displaced and reconstituted theology . . . a secularized form of devotional experience," an internalization of the Christian drama without "the dogmatic understructure of Christianity" and specifically without the redeeming love and sacrifice of Christ.[20] Unlike Milton's purpose to justify God's ways to man, the Romantic's high argument was the mind of man and all that passed within it. Thus the extremes of hell and heaven, death and rebirth were to have validity in relation only to the self who is both knower and known: the epistemological knower and the ontological known.

The contrary Calvinist notions of a sovereign and wholly other God, and of man as dependent upon divine grace, appear forgotten in Muir's own high Romantic testaments of his newness of being and paradise regained. Muir averred that divinity lies within us as we see everything in nature fitting into us: the sun shining not on us but in us, and the rivers flowing not past but through us. To know in this way, he said, is not only to see a new heaven and earth but to be born again, "as if we had gone on a pilgrimage to some far-off holy land and had become new creatures with bodies inverted."[21] Thus Muir attributes rebirth to no outside Christological event but rather to the discovery in the mind that spirit and nature are one.

Not to know oneself as part of this unity or to destroy the unity willfully through the ruination of nature, which Muir frequently associated with civilization, is to live a "fallen" condition, whereas to awaken to a preexisting oneness with nature and spirit is to be restored to new life. Of course, for the orthodox Christian the danger inherent in such Romantic mysticism is not that a person becomes one with nature but rather that he becomes God-like, a dangerous and proud delusion that negates Christ's atonement. About this all-important doctrine Muir observed, in words echoing St. Paul, that to many people it is indeed "a stumbling-block and rock of offense."[22]

As for his travels, Muir's far-off holy land in 1879 was Alaska. His posthumously published accounts, first written as journal notes, were collected in *Travels in Alaska* (1917) and *The Cruise of the Corwin* (1918). These books depict a more terrifying wildness in nature than described in his California writings; they also reveal spiritual antipodes within Muir himself.

His first excursion, an 800-mile canoe trip, sent him exploring the Alexander Archipelago, eleven hundred wooded islands forming the southeastern part of Alaska, with Samuel Hall Young, whose purpose as a Christian missionary was to locate and visit the tribes and villages of the Tlingits north and west of Wrangell with a view to establishing schools and churches. Muir's ostensible mission was to study forests, mountains, and glaciers. Whatever else he was seeking puzzled the Indians who saw Muir's campfire high on a mountainside one dark stormy night and asked Young, "Why does this strange man go into the wet woods and up the mountains on stormy nights? Why does he wander alone on barren peaks or on dangerous ice-mountains? There is no gold up there and he never takes a gun with him or a pick. *Icta mamook*—What make? Why—Why?" Why indeed except to verify nature's higher laws, which Thoreau had described as some "dull uncertain blundering purpose." Muir's apotheosis came after three days and sixty miles of paddling into Glacier Bay. There, in dangerous waters with icebergs floating everywhere, the two men looked upon Mount Fairweather at dawn, and, in Young's words, "we saw the design and purpose of it all. Now the text of the great sermon was emblazoned across the landscape—'God is love.'" Like Thoreau, who bounded from hummock to hummock, from willow root to willow root on his resurrection day, Muir leaped the crevasses of the tidewater glacier, returning in the evening to tell Young: "I've been wandering through a thousand rooms of God's crystal temple. . . . I was tempted to stay there and feast my soul, and softly freeze, until at last I would become part of the glacier. What a great death that would be!" In Muir's words the whole scene was one of "strange unearthly splendour"; it was a "holy vision." As Young and Muir paddled away, joining the outgoing bergs, " 'Gloria in excelsis' still seemed to be sounding over all the white landscape."[23]

But amid these high moments are thematic undercurrents revealing a darker side of his Romanticism. In some respects these Alaska writings contain his most somber reflections. He returned in 1880 for further exploration with Young; then in 1881 he made his third trip, this time as a member of the *Corwin,* a government ship instructed, along with its regular duties, to search in the Arctic for survivors of the missing *Jeannette* and two other lost whalers. This expedition afforded Muir the chance to see the dreary settlements in the Aleutians, on St. Lawrence Island, and along the Siberian coast. Starvation had swept many of these villages during the winter of 1878–79, and hundreds of dead lay unburied two years later. In some places where Muir and others went ashore, they saw entire villages with not a single person alive but decomposed corpses still in the huts and grinning skulls "looking out here and there." The flowering plants he was careful to find and note, even on icebound Herald Island and Wrangell Land, offer little relief to Muir's other descriptions of gray sleet, screaming water birds, howling winds, and the ever-present danger of drifting ice and unpredictable ocean currents. He also witnessed the widespread killing of walruses and seals for commercial profit, and the "butchery" of polar bears for sport. Such killing Muir called "murder," and he was continually baffled that civilized people, "seeking for heavens and angels and millenniums," enjoyed this red, brutal "amusement." The vibrant tone found in Muir's California writings is lacking in *The Cruise of the Corwin,* weighted

instead with ironic reflections about civilization and tonally
darkened by the omnipresent "black water" dashing against
the treacherous ice.[24]

What, then, of Muir's Romanticism? In time he was to
learn that more enigmatic than the heart of nature is that of
man, and that to fuse in spirit skies does not annul the old
enigmas within the human condition. With Romantic
bravado he had earlier declared that townspeople were "all
more or less sick"—that there was "not a perfectly sane man
in San Francisco." Accordingly, salvation was merely a matter of one's fleeing "as from the plague" to purer air. For
example, he had written to Mrs. Carr that whereas the tide of
visitors coming to Yosemite would "float slowly about the
bottom of the Valley as a harmless scum," he would inhabit
the rocks high above, "half way to real heaven."[25] But later
Muir would realize that half way to heaven is nothing more
than that. Life still goes on in the lowlands. And he would
involve himself in social and political service, enjoy a happy
family life with his wife, Louie Strentzel Muir, and two
daughters, become a successful rancher in Contra Costa
County, and cherish many friendships. The important point
is that later years tempered his Romanticism. The fierce old
enigmas were not to be nullified in wildness even if *there* one
has his epiphany. The Romantic self assimilates only partial
truth at best.

Although he had experienced abounding and overflowing
life, in which sickness, pain, and death seemed not to exist
because the self supposedly had merged into something
larger, Muir yet heard the bell that tolled him back to his sole
self. The fact is that he had a most uncanny premonition of it.
The event was his father's death in October, 1885. "One by
one we will join him," he mused later, even as he awaited the
first snows of winter to fall on his father's grave. The same
melancholic thought surfaced in the letter sent his wife a few
days earlier from Portage, Wisconsin, where he was visiting
old friends whose ranks were thinned by death. "As for the
old freedom I used to enjoy in the wilderness," he wrote,
"that, like youth and its enthusiasms, is evidently a thing of

the past." A new and inexorable note of *memento mori* shaded his reflections. On the occasion of his daughter's four-teenth birthday in 1895, Muir wrote in his journal, "I dread pain and trouble in so sweet and good a life. If only death and pain could be abolished!"[26] These are not the thoughts he enjoyed in the high Sierras or in Glacier Bay when death seemed like some sublime victory, some beautiful corrobora-tion of nature's eternal laws. The faint presence that now looms is not from some far-off holy region but from the grave close at hand.

What lies on this side of paradise reminded Muir of the old Christian dualism between soul and body. In spite of his affirmations about the flow and unity of nature's laws, he retained what Professor Lyon correctly identifies as a "heav-ily dualized Christian cosmogony." "Soul and body," Muir wrote, "receive separate nourishment and separate exercise, and speedily reach a stage of development wherein each is easily known apart from the other." Soul was the divine spark known in a rapt state of wildness; body was the bondage of society and mortality, symbolized by life in the lowlands. Muir realized that the claims of both soul and body need to be answered. To turn away from human society in hopes of achieving spiritual purity denied the claims of time and place and denied as well the need for human love. "In all God's mountain mansions," Muir said, "I find no human sympathy, and I hunger." In wildness the soul comes to know a certain weariness that the lowlands, for all their ills, can alleviate.[27]

Revealed in Muir's seasoned thoughts is the ever-present duality between soul and body, nature's wildness and human society, future and past, God and man. His Romantic expec-tations that in each case the former could become all in all in the latter failed to obliterate the deep Calvinist sense of hu-man finitude and appalling contingency. To soar with elevated thoughts changed not a whit the retributive reminder that sickness, pain, and death pervade the only life one really knows, and human love and divine grace afford its only hope.

Muir's travels did not abate, but his accounts of them reflect an imagination less spontaneous and empyrean. In

1893 he saw John Burroughs in New York and dined with
Gilder. In Concord he dined with Emerson's son, Edward
Waldo, laid flowers on Emerson's and Thoreau's graves,
went to Walden Pond, and visited Nathaniel Hawthorne's
Old Manse. In Boston he saw Josiah Royce and Francis Park-
man, and in Manchester, forty miles away, Sarah Orne
Jewett. He also returned to his old home in Dunbar, Scotland. In 1896 he received an honorary degree at Harvard, in
1897 another at the University of Wisconsin. In 1898 he
tramped through the Alleghenies; in 1903 he took a world
tour; in 1911 he sailed up the Amazon and also to Africa. Of
all these travels the most impressive was his return to Scotland
in 1893, a journey into the past, there to remember the lessons his father had taught him. Still touched by their power,
he wrote from Dunbar to his daughter Wanda, "Ask mother
to give you lessons to commit to memory every day. Mostly
the sayings of Christ in the gospels and selections from the
poets. Find the hymn of praise in *Paradise Lost* 'These are thy
glorious works, Parent of Good, Almighty,' and learn it
well."[28]

In what I have called Muir's "seasoned thoughts," especially as they occur in his later journals, there is a Calvinist
tone pointing to a world that nature does not symbolize, that
a writer's consciousness does not assimilate, that his word can
never record. At times this realm is terrifying, at other times
benign. Mystery, the *mysterium tremendum,* is at the heart of
it, a mystery Muir frequently called "glorious." Friends
chided him for overusing the adjective; the same complaint
could be made against Jonathan Edwards. For both, the word
signified the ineffable mystery that opens the eye not only to
see but to behold: in short, a mystery that inheres in and acts
upon men and nature.

For Muir the writer, his closing years, from the time of his
wife's death in 1905 to his own nine years later, sent him
more and more into the past and into an inner world even
while he roamed the outer. His earlier reluctance to write
about himself now gave way to a sense of urgency. He applied himself, according to Badè, "too unremittingly" for his

own health.[29] His effort now was to reach within himself and, using notes written long years earlier, to make public the private spiritual drama associated with that first remarkable summer in the Sierras. He also probed into his boyhood and youth in an effort to understand the shaping influences there. These two autobiographical journeys—*My First Summer in the Sierra* and *The Story of My Boyhood and Youth*—show Muir looking back to a time when powerful crosscurrents of ideas and experiences were shaping his developing self. Considered along with his other writings, these books also show Muir wishing to complete what had always been his great themes: nature, the self, and the divine mystery infusing both with ultimate meaning. Celebrating all three indicated that the earlier crosscurrents had never really subsided.

Had he lived longer he would have written more of the autobiographical things he had wanted to say. As it was, he spent his ripened days reading old notes, arranging them on the floor, he said, "like lateral, medial, and terminal moraines." The image affords a picture of the interior landscape that Muir was now traversing, still treasuring the longings for communion, the symbols of salvation, and the assurance of a sovereign and absolute power exceeding the reaches of self. On Christmas Eve, the day of his death in Los Angeles, he was still traveling those moraines. This time they were his Alaska notes spread out before him on his bed. In one of his last journal notations, he had described the nature of this final excursion: "I only went out for a walk, and finally concluded to stay out till sundown, for going out, I found, was really going in."[30]

That Muir showed his reader the Sierras more vividly than anyone else has done; that he worked successfully for their natural preservation; that his sense of joyful wildness still provides an antidote for today's quiet desperation make us all his debtors. We are also indebted for his going down into those inner peaks and valleys that call for a different kind of courage. There within, John Muir fronted the essential facts of life and death, and showed us what it means to be a true frontiersman. Muir reached the edges of experience, his visionary eye beholding all things as linked to one another. It must be said, however, that Muir had a darker side—a recurring sense of mortality, discordance, and judgment—that intermingled with his Romanticism, deepened and enriched it, and enhanced his searching literary consciousness. The clear Sierra waters, reflecting in his writing a limitless sky, also made their subterranean connections not only with a Romanticist's Walden but with the dark and treacherous ocean eddies that swirled around the rocks where Muir as a Scottish child had sat and meditated about his father's teachings.

5
Terror and Defensive Stratagems in Robert Frost

I

Among the last and most eminent of America's philosophical idealists was Josiah Royce, born in Grass Valley, California, the same year Whitman published *Leaves of Grass* (1855). He finished high school in San Francisco, received his undergraduate degree from the University of California, and then, after study in Germany and elsewhere in the United States, went to Harvard in 1882, where he remained the rest of his life as a professor of philosophy. In 1912, four years before his death, his Bross Lectures were published on *The Sources of Religious Insight,* the last chapter of which Sydney E. Ahlstrom regards as a résumé of the entire series "if not his whole life work."[1] Entitled "The Unity of the Spirit and the Invisible Church," Royce's summation posited two kinds of consciousness. One is "natural" consciousness by which we grasp facts and ideas but only in a severely limited way. If confined only to natural consciousness we live within an intolerable narrowness, doomed to have merely "instantaneous glimpses" of truth but never a wider outlook. Fortunately, however, the very restriction forces us to rebel, and in rebellion to see things "*not* through these instantaneous cracks, but without intervening walls, with wide outlook, and in all their true variety and unity." Raising the issue to its highest urgency, Royce insisted that "salvation itself is at

stake in this struggle for a wider clearness of outlook." Because no mortal person ever directly possesses this view, we
must live, despite our narrowness, "*as if* we saw widely." To
do this we "indirectly" escape from limitation by means of
"generalization or abstraction" such as only a different kind
of consciousness can realize. This second consciousness he
called "superhuman," which includes all our insights but
"transcends and corrects" them and establishes a "unity of
meaning," a supernatural harmony in which we all live. No
special grace, signs, miracles, or wonders are needed to prove
this unity. "Common-sense tacitly presupposes the reality of
the unity of the spirit"; reason gives us insight into its real
being; and "salvation means our positive harmony with its
purpose and with its manifestation." Royce's keynote
affirmation is that this unity of spirit is the essence of spiritual
brotherhood, itself a true community in which its members
are devoted "to bringing themselves into harmony with the
purposes of the universe." Such a brotherhood, essentially
religious in its nature, is the real church whether the group be
that of family, business, or nation. Joined together by the
love and loyalty of its members, the community Royce envisioned is "to be a city set on a hill."[2]

　　How much of John Muir's high Sierra sunlight that also
had freshened Royce's spirit still remained with the
philosopher in Boston we can only surmise, taking note of
the contrast between the city he envisioned set upon a hill and
the one the Puritans hoped for in the selfsame Boston. Coming to Boston two and a half centuries later, Royce brought
with him a different principle. His was a Romantic philosophy, a metaphysics of integration of which the key principle,
at least as old as Neoplatonic thought, was the synthesis of
whatever is divided, conflicting, and discontinuous. Perhaps
Royce can be seen as an archetypal Westerner who returns to
the place from which he once set forth. The Westerner's journey had been a symbolic process of reconciling the old divi-
sions of nature and spirit, a process in the reintegration of
self. Whereas the Puritans had conceived their course to be a
Heilsgeschichte,　　the　　American　　Westerner　　transformed

theological history into the secular mode of *Bildungsge-schichte*—that is, the education *(Bildung)* of the mind from a lower to a higher consciousness and thus to a triumphant apotheosis, in which the purpose of the universe is internalized.[3] The old Christian wayfarer on his pilgrimage to the heaven-haven of Boston had become the Western hero and mystic who, bearing no cross, travel through stages of awareness culminating in the vision of a new city untouched by grace and unfettered by covenant. It is a city whose members have been graduated into self-enlightenment and whose common citizenship is not their old sins but their newfound divinity.

Royce's idealism infused liberal Christianity with an optimism that Walter Rauschenbusch translated into the hope for a kingdom of brotherly love and social equality on earth. Both the philosophical idealism and the subsequent social Gospel partook of basic Romantic assumptions about the nature of man. Noteworthy is the fact that both spokesmen, Royce and Rauschenbusch, were spared through death the full impact of the Great War. However, even with the dawning of the "troglodyte world," in which millions slaughtered one another in the trenches of France, these Romantic assumptions were slow to die, if indeed they have died at all.[4] Screams of holocausts merely added aesthetic decadence to songs a later generation was to sing about Aquarius. To theologians Karl Barth and the Niebuhr brothers (H. Richard and Reinhold) the horror of historical events confirmed a preexisting darkness of the human spirit, not to be dispelled by a superhuman consciousness playing the game of "as if" but only by a supernatural grace. What lay beyond the broken walls of civilization, shockingly visible, was the darkling plain of ignorant armies—and, beyond that, a world where either faith or utter hopelessness is born.

Robert Frost was also a Californian who spent some of his boyhood in San Francisco and went east, ending north of Boston. Only eleven at the time he left in 1885, he nevertheless carried with him intimations vastly different from those that had nurtured Royce. Years later these feelings revealed a deep terror pervading his whole life. Contrary to apotheosis, his western vision was that of great ocean waves under "low and hairy" clouds, the waves originating not from a principle of unity but from some monstrous and elemental force of "dark intent." The land proved only illusory safety against their menacing finality ("Once by the Pacific").[5] In Frost's vision a threat inevitably appeared from beyond the shore, behind the wall, or beneath the surface of a dappled pond. Its menacing nature bore testimony to the violence certain to occur once the truth is known. Like an assailant, this "something" will shatter inherited assumptions and benign expectations. Doing total violence to these securities, it will reveal itself as no truth at all, at least in no absolute sense, and will confirm the spaces to be utterly bereft of purpose and meaning. Preoccupied, as it were, to get beyond the frontier, Frost experienced the terror of finding nothing, often perversely (and proudly) calling this discovery a victory and then setting about desperately to build protective defenses against the terror.

In an exhaustive analysis Norman N. Holland shows how Matthew Arnold set about doing the same, especially in "Dover Beach," a poem replete with moral, psychological, and aesthetic soothings until the final two lines come crashing in upon our consciousness. According to Holland, Victorians needed all the protection they could get.[6] Also needing the protection that ego and art provide, Frost structured personas and poems as stratagems to heal a consciousness all but shattered by the knowledge of a "dark intent." Frost was an artist who, whether or not he valued Romantic assumptions about human nature, wagered his highest stakes upon the self and its creative imagination to structure a reality absolute and privileged. In playing out the consequences of the wager, he had no choice but to make terror the mover of his art.

II

It is not for me to know why Lionel Trilling chose Robert Frost's eighty-fifth birthday celebration as the occasion to call him a "terrifying poet." As it turned out, Trilling's speech struck as discordant a note as did Mark Twain's on the occasion of Whittier's eightieth birthday. But whereas Twain erred on the side of jest, Trilling spoke of things too weighty, saying in the packed Waldorf-Astoria banquet room that Frost's popularly loved poetry depicts a "terrifying universe." As if to compound the effrontery, he added that American readers (presumably including the assembled guests) lacked the courage to face the "terrible actualities" comprising Frost's world. Americans can only dodge. They are the greatest dodgers because (here Trilling quotes D. H. Lawrence) "they dodge their own very selves." Of course Trilling was not so perverse as to say outright that Frost's popularity—represented by forty-four honorary degrees, four Pulitzer Prizes, numerous distinguished medals, and congressional and presidential recognition—stemmed from widespread misunderstanding of his poetry. Nor did he say that if his poetry had been read aright, no such celebration, no such panoply of honors, would now grace this name. Yet the published denunciations excoriated Trilling for what he had said. He had hit a nerve, and he had done so with unacceptable audacity. After all, this was to have been an occasion when the legendary Frost was to sit like a reassuring presence among celebrating admirers and a satisfied publisher.[7]

What Trilling had seen and what he suspected too many readers had not seen in Frost's poetry was terror. The term is saved from cant by the confessional tone that Trilling risked when, in summoning personal testimony, he spoke about "my Frost." As for the shock that rippled through the audience, Trilling wrote off the event as merely a "cultural episode." One suspects, however, that he intended a remarkably confessional essay, "On the Teaching of Modern Literature," published two years later, to serve as an aftermath. In this essay he recounts how the routine ways of literary criticism failed to serve when he himself came to teach such moderns as Yeats, Eliot, Joyce, Proust, Kafka, Lawrence, Mann, and Gide. Merely to examine these writers in a *"literary"* way, to do formal analysis, to discuss structure, went against his grain because such analysis, he said, presupposed structures of words as static and commemorative, not mobile and aggressive, and failed to take into account how much *"damage"* they can do. Although Trilling stops short of confessing to damage, he does emphasize how these writers invade the "intimacies of one's own feelings" and ask us "if we are content with ourselves, if we are saved or damned." For more than with anything else, Trilling asserted, modern literature is concerned with salvation.[8]

Even though he does not mention Frost in this essay, the terror earlier alluded to is the same that Trilling finds in these other modern writers whom his students at Columbia demanded be included in the college syllabus. Trilling obliged, saying, in effect, let the students have their gay and easy time, let them write their term papers, let them be entertained by the terror, let them look into the abyss and hear its voice say, "Interesting, am I not? And *exciting,* if you consider how deep I am and what dread beasts lie at my bottom."[9] Trilling knew the students would contain the attack. No alien element would damage their old deities whom they worship in "peace and unawareness." The only dread beasts would be the ones threatening a grade point average. Furthermore, what possible damage could come from poems written by someone honored with forty-four academic degrees?

Why Frost hungered and thirsted after these honors is a matter we can put aside, though it is not irrelevant. The concern now is the terror, for Trilling is correct in identifying Frost's "ultimate radicalism" as not just the disintegration of the old Romantic consciousness, including the old pieties of copybook and counting house, but also the terror that remains. That this is the alien element making Frost American, in a way many Americans fail to recognize, is the same irony that nineteenth-century readers missed in Hawthorne, Melville, and Twain. That which radically contradicts the Western apotheosis is no less American. No matter that when readers glimpse the terror, they turn away in disgust, unable to accommodate the alien vision. Time still bestows recognition and even greatness to American artists whose impulse is, in fact, most American when it belies the American gods!

Speculating about terror in American literature, however, is hardly the same as seeking the beasts in someone's heart. Hawthorne and Henry James have given fair warning to all biographical critics. Yet what do we do with Lawrance Thompson's monumental biography of Frost but use it, and quicken at its dreadful litany documenting the cry in Frost's own poem, "Home Burial": "I'm cursed. God, if I don't believe I'm cursed."

Young Frost and his sister were cursed by fear. Thompson says they drank it with their mother's milk. Their father, who died when Robbie was eleven, was often violent and drunk. After his death in San Francisco, their bereft mother took them east to live off relatives. In the inexorable years that followed, sister Jeanie died in a Maine asylum for the insane and their mother died of cancer. After Robert Frost's marriage to Elinor White, their firstborn son died of cholera at the age of four; a daughter died later in infancy. Elinor herself died from a series of heart attacks following surgery for breast cancer. Of the four surviving children, Lesley married, was divorced, and later refused her father's request to live in her house after her mother died; Carol, the son, whose wife, Lillian, contracted tuberculosis, committed suicide; Irma married, was divorced, and suffered paranoid delusions in a New Hampshire mental hospital; and Marjorie, who suffered a nervous breakdown, died the same year her only child was born. Perhaps it is not amiss to note parenthetically that Frost's long and best friend, Louis Untermeyer, suffered his own miserere that included four marriages and the suicide of his son at Yale. Not surprising is Frost's admission to his sympathetic friend: "I sometimes take it pretty hard to be left in a city apartment alone with the night."[10] Not surprising also is Frost's fascination with the Book of Job.

The days that darkened around him, especially after Elinor's death in 1938, compounded his sense of failure in the way he had brought up his children. He concluded he had "taught them more fear than courage" (2:497). Even worse was his sense of guilt toward Elinor. Not only had his "passionate demands" brought her six children when even from the first the doctor had warned of her weak heart, but he had mocked her pessimism, deceiving her for his own "selfish pleasure" by pretending he thought the world a better place than she. Her death now seemed like a sacrifice to prove her argument and to bring him down. "I know," he confessed, "I never had a leg to stand on, and I should think I had said so in print" (2:501). Guilt for denigrating her deepest feelings and then for saying he had had "almost too much of her suffering in this world" (2:486) confirmed what he asked in "A Question": whether "all the soul-and-body scars / Were not too much to pay for birth." Elinor's refusal to see him during her final hours was the price he paid for her death. Indeed, the nerve Lionel Trilling hit by saying that Frost exposed the terrifying things of human life may have been the nerve of the honored guest himself who, flustered and discomposed after Trilling had finished his remarks, conceded, "I'm nervous tonight, I'm very nervous. . . . I haven't been given to think about myself so much in my whole life" (3:269). On the contrary, poems like "Storm Fear," "Tree at My Window," "Acquainted with the Night," and "Desert Places" reveal he had given much thought to himself. And in each he was afraid.

The problem for Frost was always one of strategy: what to do with the night and the nightmares, the woods and the snow and the haunting presences like the one in "The Demiurge's Laugh" that mocked and beguiled him, or in "Storm Fear" that beckoned him to "Come out! Come out!" into the dark. The fact that throughout his life he wanted to associate himself with heroic adventurers failed to mitigate his fear, and makes understandable his insatiable desire for public recognition. To have a closet full of academic hoods allows little room for anything else. What served most readily was a public persona even at the price of self-deception, nagging falsehoods, and emotional vicissitudes hidden behind the façade. His stubborn ambition to succeed as a poet by gaining the widest possible approbation grew into a private war, a more exciting affair for Frost in 1914 than the other war heating up in Europe. He became an expert in manipulating people for his own ends, using gossip as a "bladelike weapon" (2:xvii), and not hesitating to hone it by altering facts. Jealous of contemporaries like Edwin Arlington Robinson and Edgar Lee Masters whose reputations threatened to eclipse his own, he sought vengeance upon those who rejected his work. Furthermore, he spurned Irving Babbitt and the other Humanists, derided Carl Sandburg, slandered Bernard De-Voto, loathed the writings of William Faulkner and said so, excoriated the "Pound-Eliot-Richards' gang," hated F. O. Matthiessen and his "crowd" of leftist critics, belittled his Amherst colleagues Professor Stark Young and President Alexander Meiklejohn. All this and more resonate in Thompson's biography. What needs noting is that Frost's aim in this private war was to triumph publicly as a homespun, New England farmer-poet pretending only casual concern about his growing success.

Unprecedented in twentieth-century American letters, Frost's success as poet-entertainer brought him prizes, medals, distinguished awards and memberships, and always the overflow public audiences solemnly assembled to hear his seasoned wisdom. He read poems that sometimes showed him a philosophical dualist, other times a monist; sometimes a humanist and other times a theist; one time the advocate of moral acquiescence, another time of resistance and outrage. Sometimes the tone was acerbic, ironic, or whimsical; other times duly solemn. Then his caveat: "Don't trust me too far. I'm liable to tell you anything. Trust me on the poetry, but don't trust me on my life" (1:xiv). The bromide works if poetry claims ultimate authority, and if ambiguity serves only an aesthetic strategy. But whether the poem, which Frost in "The Revelation" designated as a "place apart," can embrace the ambiguities of the heart creates enough misgivings to make precarious the security that art and its public triumph afford.

What Frost in this same poem calls the "agitated heart"

contravenes the stratagems to quiet it. Like Emily Dickinson's "bandaged soul," the inmost region of the self knows a terror both beautiful and lethal, beguiling and offensive. Frost's terror points to something behind nature's pastoral benignity. In "For Once, Then, Something" he identifies this presence as "something" once perceived in the depths of a well—"something white, uncertain" that momentarily appeared beyond and through his own reflected face and then forever disappeared in an obtrusive ripple. Its whiteness augurs that of the "dimpled spider, fat and white" in Frost's chilling poem, "Design." In both poems a Melvillian whiteness makes appalling its ambiguous dark design. Again Frost introduces this "something" in "Mending Wall"; he flaunts it in a repeated line: "Something there is that doesn't love a wall." Thoughts about how neighbors behave toward each other deflect our attention from the main business of the poem, which concerns the walling out of some malignant agency or force that vexes us by spilling our protective stones. The destructive agent is not the old stone-savage neighbor. More primal than the neighbor's instinct to build walls is something that would destroy the walls and have at us.

Frost's maneuver in "Triple Bronze" is wholly defensive: to build a wall between "too much and me." Now the threat is infinity itself. For the American Romantics who welcomed the infinite, walls were a great waste of stone and mortar. Thoreau and Whitman would have none of them—would stride confidently beyond them, meet the infinite, and make it theirs. In "The Most of It," however, Frost had only to send his voice abroad, hoping for some corresponding voice, some "counter-love" and "original response," to discover instead the dreadful truth that nothing exists out there but the "mocking echo" of his own voice, grotesquely transfigured into some giant buck now thrashing its way through the underbrush towards him.

The immensity of space is a vast nothingness one moment and a menacing force the next. To one speaker in the title poem of *West-Running Brook* (1928) infinity is the "abyss' void"; and existence—including time, strength, tone, light, and love—is the brook flowing west "to fill" the void with "emptiness." The brook flows over, between, with us, ending as a "universal cataract of death/That spends to nothing-ness." Again oriented westward in "Once by the Pacific," the poet shudders with apocalyptic terror as he beholds the menacing waves intent upon his annihilation. And again the question: What to do? Build a wall? Risk the journey to the edge of the howling infinite, there to gaze but not too far out or in too deep? Or yield to annihilation?

The beckoning knock at the door, like that of Poe's raven, insists upon attention ("The Lockless Door"); the face appearing in the dark bushes will not be abstracted ("The Fear"); the thrush's song is "almost like a call" to enter the dark woods ("Come In"); indeed, the woods are "lovely, dark and deep" ("Stopping by Woods on a Snowy Evening"). As if overtaken by the end, Frost was tempted to yield to death as the only surcease from terror. His son's suicide showed the way. To Frost the dismal swamp was anything but a Thoreauvian *sanctum sanctorum.* Its wildness, in which such as Thoreau and Muir thought was to be found the pres-ervation of the world, suggested a contrary destructiveness or at best a peaceful annihilation. Thoreau's dismal swamp was Frost's dark woods that "stretched away unto the edge of doom." Nearly forty when he wrote these words, which ap-pear in the first poem of his earliest volume, *A Boy's Will* (1913), Frost stood on the edge of the Dantesque woods. "Into My Own" announces their vastness in which, for his remaining years, he longed to steal away.

Repeatedly Frost's poems testify to the soul's dark night where "black bats" tumble ("Ghost House") and where one's straight way is lost amid the "desolate, deserted trees" ("My November Guest") and the "tangle of withered weeds" ("A Late Walk"). Like Melville's ocean or the immigrant Ole Röl-vaag's western prairie, the woods shadow forth a compelling demonism. The inherent terror within nature preempts all else. Although the will resists annihilation, the woods com-mand the heart to own its emptiness. "Leaves must go down past things coming up," Frost writes in "In Hardwood

Groves"; "they must go down into the dark decayed." Observing nature's cycle does not assuage human fear nor inform the heart untouched by death. The fallen leaf must first be pierced before the flowers grow. A person learns by going where the woods command.

Frost refuses to presuppose sacramentalism in nature's power, and he finds no redemption in its wildness. Nature answers no questions and solves no problems. It cares nothing for families, lives, or human affairs. In Frost's desperate little narrative entitled "The Birthplace," we make a clearing on nature's mountain slopes, we find a spring and build some walls, we subdue the earth to grass, and then we rear a family. And for awhile the mountain "seemed" to like the stir. But "something in her smile" strikes terror in our reverence. Inevitably the mountain pushes "us off her knees./And now her lap is full of trees." "No more to build on there" is the ambiguous summation in "'Out, Out—'." Neither reverence nor love withstands the encircling doom. The heroic choice to yield or not to yield gives way to primal emotions of desire and hate, and they in turn prove puny whims before the coming of fire or ice.

Every structure Frost created—whether a public mask, a household, or a poem—had terrifying vacancies that public triumphs barely stretched across to hide. Protection afforded by the created form or public honor was never more than momentary, thus compelling him to create again and again or to seek still more reassurances that the world thought well of him. It was a precarious game. In accepting the gold medal of the National Institute of Arts and Letters in 1939 he said he hoped the medal signified he had "fitted" into the American scene.[11] But his poem, "One Step Backward Taken," opens vacancies too vast to hide. High on the dizzy edge of fame the poet has the perverse impulse not only to plunge to his death but to do some forbidden act, to do the very thing he hates. About this Pauline perversity Poe wrote, "If there be no friendly arm to check us, or if we fail in a sudden effort to prostrate ourselves backward from the abyss, we plunge, and are destroyed."[12]

Imagery in "One Step Backward Taken" recalls that of Paul Tillich in *The Shaking of the Foundation.* An earthquake nudges great boulders "off their balance" and sends them bumping down the gully while "whole capes" cake off in slices. In all Frost's poetry nothing identifies the nexus of terror better than the two lines that follow: "I felt my standpoint shaken/In the universal crisis." Yet even this frightful vision accompanying Frost during his honored years was not without a certain guile, suggested in the bold assertion: "But with one step backward taken/I saved myself from going." (More accurately, the friendly arm of Mrs. Kathleen Morrison saved him. But in justice to Frost, one must cite his beautiful poem, "A Silken Tent," written with her in mind.)

Saved from what ("A world torn loose went by me") bespeaks a clearer answer than the question, Saved *for* what? Saved to keep "promises" is the ambiguous reply in his most famous poem. The essential question, however, is neither from what nor for what but *by whom,* and here the answer is unambiguous: "I saved myself." The residual Romanticism that Frost espoused finds its meaning in consciousness alone. Jonathan Edwards would have mitigated the terror in this isolation by affirming a slender thread joining man and God. No thread exists in Frost's poem. The "I" stands alone to work out its own salvation or be lost.

That many critics applaud Frost at this point for his flint-hard stoicism and endurance does not make less persuasive the varied arguments of others who attack him. Among his so-called negative critics one theme predominates: Frost lacked the courage to explore where his vision led. The tragic power promised in his early volumes finds only timid handling later (Bogan). A "spiritual drifter," Frost treats the major theme of life and death, good and evil, and moral choice in a "whimsical, sentimental, and evasive" manner, such that "an obscure melancholy which he can neither control nor understand" pervades his later poetry (Winters). Frost's condition of survival is "strategic withdrawal" (Pearce). The later Frost "makes demands on himself that are minimal" (Jarrell). His criticism of life is "merely poetic" (Carpenter). He is

attacked by others for his social and political conservatism
(Arvin, Humphries, Cowley, Howe), and the critics probing
the existential Frost have found ambivalence, bad faith, and
failure of nerve.[13]

The most thoroughgoing of these critics is George W.
Nitchie, who finds in Frost an "incompleteness" revealed not
only in tendencies toward "the arch or the snide or the oracu-
lar" but also in a refusal "to be pinned down." Frost preferred
to play the Yankee character, to destroy straw men, to be
querulous and cranky—"the gestures of one who is not sure
where he stands and who finds it increasingly difficult to
make adequate compensation for that fundamental uncertainty."[14] Instead of tragic struggle or an overruling myth we
are to see in Frost only canny adjustment. We are given only
the theme of a single poem or the position of isolated individuals in a world they seldom attempt to understand. There
is, Nitchie argues, a sense in which Frost is not really serious
about his poetry and the convictions it embodies. Serious as
this indictment is, it rings true to Thompson's insistence that
Frost "hid his uncertainties behind contradictions which
baffled others, and he could at least enjoy the protection thus
gained" (1:xiv–xv). The point concerns not so much the poet
as the man. Whatever the artistic achievement of the one, the
moral life of the other must have its due. Poe knew the terror
in the dichotomy when the poet is not the man, when the two
make two, not one. For Frost, public prizes served to authen-
ticate the one identity, even on his deathbed when he received
the Bollingen Prize. As for the other identity, he stood sup-
ported by little more than an uncertain pride in his independence and the bardic wisdom that supposedly issued from it.

The critics I have mentioned reveal nothing Frost himself
was not aware of, though he refused to read most of them and
in his later years was positively protected from them by Mrs.
Morrison. Indeed the theme persists too incessantly for anyone to doubt Frost's psychic peril or to mistake the voice in
The Masque of Reason (1945) when the Keeper confesses the
lack of courage "to overcome the fear within the soul." This
fear lying at the root of things is the dread of existence itself,

evoked not by this or that event, place, or state of affairs within the world, but by the total situation of being human; it is the precarious position between what a person is and what he projects himself to be or is obliged to become. In this delicate balance choice as a condition of being takes on definitive significance. In "Trial by Existence" Frost affirms that life not only consists of the things we have chosen but is the act of choice itself, forever juxtaposed with dread and thus forever "stripped of pride."

To write poems about choice is one thing, to make fundamental choices and live accordingly is another. The point of reference for the first is aesthetic beauty and poetic productivity; whereas the second calls for a mode of existence based not on aesthetic stratagems but on moral and religious convictions. For the poet as poet, choice is the freedom to say one thing in one poem, another in another, and both poems can "work" equally well aesthetically. Frost, the poet, can speak of the trial by existence, saying in the poem that choice is the "essence of life"; but in another poem ("Acceptance") the theme is "Let what will be, be." The two themes can conjoin in still another poem: the heart aches to seek, yet its wisdom is only to know "the drift of things, / To yield . . . bow . . . accept" ("Reluctance"). Each poem succeeds as a poem. In each the poet's imagination has shaped the initial perception while also allowing it to assume its inherent direction. The poem is a finished structure, an ordered thing, an aesthetic resolution, a felicitous integration. What begins in delight and inclines to impulse supposedly ends in wisdom, in "a clarification of life," though Frost immediately qualifies this grandiose assertion by acknowledging that the so-called clarification is hardly what "sects and cults" are founded on but rather is, at best, only a "momentary stay against confusion." What then is clarified? Frost does not say. His apparent answer is life as an aesthetic thing, not as the moral and spiritual world he identifies only as "the vast chaos of all I have lived through."[15] Certainly the chaos has not been clarified for either himself or his reader. In the meantime the poet, like a playful bear, is free to sit back "on his fundamental butt" and sway from cheek to cheek, "At one extreme agreeing with one Greek [Plato the idealist]/At the other agreeing with another Greek [Democritus the materialist]" ("The Bear").[16]

The figure a poem makes may have nothing to do with the figure a person makes. Poetic modes originate in imagination and reasoned strategy. To trust the poem, as Frost admonishes, is hardly the total commitment, the risk, the leap required to trust the person or, on the religious level, the divine. Trust on this ultimate level originates in choice that centers in existence, integrates being and doing, and eventuates in a faith that costs everything. The distinction is between poet and person, revealed time and again in Frost who, as a poet, wrote about humility of spirit while his other self hungered for glory. Rarely interested in any performances but his own, he boasted, "I only go when I'm the show" (2:424).

These thoughts suggest that for Frost the nature of art was urgently defensive. Art was a stratagem for coping with existence. It provided momentary stay against the threat of psychological and spiritual destruction, insanity, and suicide. Thompson speculates that Frost used his poems most of the time "as tools or as weapons for actually trying to bring under control and resolve those conflicts which he viewed as being so dangerous that they might otherwise engulf and destroy him" (1:xxii). Writing poetry thus became a "saving action" (2:xix). In a sense Frost confirmed these insights when he answered Granville Hicks's review of *Collected Poems* (1930). To Hicks's charge that he had failed to cope with the chaotic elements within his own inner world Frost replied that against the "black and utter chaos . . . any small manmade figure of order" is welcome (2:388). The charge begs for a deeper answer, but Frost's reply settles only for artistic design. The road Frost declined to follow, even though he saw its direction, would have taken him deep within himself. He chose instead the road taking him to the supreme fiction, to the poetic act, which in its achieved stasis momentarily resists a vastly greater instability.

The road that Frost did not choose wound into the deeper woods where passage is successful only when a person trusts human relationships and, in the deepest extremity, a divine one. Here is the landscape where courage is tested and real choices are made. Of the two roads that diverged in the woods, Frost chose the one that led to the clearing where he could play his desperate game of rhymes and meters, trusting language to obviate the greater entanglements. The clearing defined Frost's world of art. It was its own ontology, hierarchical and privileged. It was the world of "as if" where artifices serve as one's salvation, where stratagems replace choices, where artists live in their "place apart" and grow into consummate dodgers. The clearing was the farm where Frost could live by writing poems and call that farming. It was, he says in "Build Soil," where

> I prefer to sing safely in the realm
> Of types, composite and imagined people:
> To affirm there is such a thing as evil
> Personified, but ask to be excused
> From saying on a jury, 'Here's the guilty.'

Judgments made by critics are rarely as damning as those made by one's closest friends and family. The first kind Frost could handle by returning like for like; the second left him stunned, most notably when, after Elinor's death, his daughter Lesley refused him permission to live with her family. She said she had seen him injure the lives of his own children—particularly Irma, Carol, and Marjorie—and she did not want him to do the same to her own two daughters. Through tears of rage she insisted he had ruined her mother's life also. Then, according to Thompson, "she hurt him most by concluding that he was the kind of artist who never should have married, or at least never should have had a family." As between art and family, she knew what her father's choice had been. His own feelings of guilt indicated a private admission as well, but in moments of impatience and self-vindication he maintained that "his devotion to his art had been spoiled by his devotion to his family" (2:495, 496).

The whole distasteful business signals the kind of dilemma many artists face. Moreover, it suggests something of the dualism that inheres in art between its being a closed and nonreferential world of meaning and, on the other hand, an entity that windows existence and is informed by it. The artist who follows the imperatives of the first takes from experience what serves the dramatic rquirements of his art. He makes an illusory order, a separate peace. Although the aesthetic soundness of his creation might symbolize a larger moral and cosmic soundness, the fact remains that symbol and poem are his own artifices and his alone. According to Frost, the achievement constitutes "a new order with not so much as a ligature clinging to it of the old place."[17] If, on the other hand, the artist follows the imperatives of the second, he knows that artistic form must yield to his deeper self. A roar penetrates the silence of the well-wrought artifice and gives notice of a raw, archaic place anterior to the poem and, for the reader, posterior to it as well. The voice comes deep from a moral and spiritual consciousness, fuses with a similar consciousness of the reader, and in mutual trust makes artist and literary critic human beings before they are either the one or the other. First as persons, both artist and reader look full-face upon the anarchical element, accept it as part and parcel of themselves, and then walk as before but with this shared knowledge forever their own.

With Frost the stakes get high in betting on poetry to keep the clearing open. The question continually obtrudes whether the order and symmetry in art reflect a corresponding self. Balance is a major theme in Frost: balance in art, in nature's cycles, in human reason; balance between good and evil, faith and reason, justice and mercy, plus all the balanced symbols that Frost uses. The theme receives humorous treatment in "The Armful," and more psychological and metaphysical treatment in "Two Tramps in Mud Time," "Birches," and "To Earthward." The theme pervades the two masques. It also reflects Frost's own compulsive need for balance, bearing upon the persistent dichotomy between the figure a poem makes and that which a person makes, and the Dimmesdale-

Clues aplenty had foretold the catastrophe: that an ever-expanding consciousness brought with it its own despair, which in turn compelled the self to ever-greater strides against a ceaseless current. The Romanticism that created the self destroyed the self. Self-trust that lacked the slender thread was its own destructive element, its own final laugh in the vacant immensity.

Hayden Carruth argues that no laugh in Hawthorne, James, and Robinson matches the laugh in Frost's "The Vanishing Red," a poem that Carruth thinks reflects the center of Frost's poetic temperament: "the blackest, bitterest despair in three hundred years of New England tradition."[19] In the poem a Red Man named John, curious about the flour mill's wheel-pit, is led below by the miller, who lifts the manhole on the floor, shows John "the water in desperate straits like frantic fish," returns upstairs *alone*, and gives "that laugh." "Oh, yes," the poet concludes, "he showed John the wheel-pit all right." Of the old Romantic consciousness that once journeyed forth, all that now remains tells only of the black water, the frantic beings in it, and the satanic heart of him who laughs to send another into its desperate straits.

Might not the miller be the poet? André Gide said it well in his little book on Dostoevsky: "The Fiend is a party to every work of art."[20] When the poet is the archcreator and all existence serves his art, the sacrifice is someone else's. However, in the end it is the poet's own heart. For like Faust he has chosen not to love but to know, not to live but to create.

6
Art, Humanism, and Christian Consciousness

I

One line of argument in the preceding chapters concerns the perils facing the Romantic hero, whether artist or frontiersman, who wagers that his achievements of imagination, will, and spirit will vindicate his natural limitations. Rebellious toward whatever restricts the flowering of these endowments, or anxious about the possible meaninglessness of his existence, he concentrates mightily upon his self-worth. He dreams imperial dreams about himself; he universalizes his importance; he absorbs himself into the infinite; he creates works having the appearance of unconditional reality in order to keep at bay the conditional, contingent, and dependent nature of his existence. He wagers that his power to conquer, to assimilate, or to create will be all-sufficient. In the meantime, intruding into his consciousness is the fearful possibility that the greater he becomes, the greater the risk of his destruction.

The judgment is a religious one, going back, for example, to Isaiah: "Thy wisdom and thy knowledge, it hath perverted thee; and thou hast said in thine heart, I am, and none else beside me" (Isa. 47:10). Ezekiel castigates pride and self-sufficiency. Psalm 49 inveighs against false security. St. Paul's definition of sin issues from this same prophetic interpretation, namely, that sinful man seeks to make himself God (Rom. 1:18–22). The perils of self-consciousness including all its human ramifications are those of pride, sin, damnation, and destruction. Other themes in western civilization have vied with this one, but none has permanently eclipsed it. Pride is what Augustine called "a perverse desire of height"; it is when the soul "likes itself too well"—or, again, "when the soul abandons Him to which it ought to cleave as its end and becomes a kind of end in itself." In Pascal's definition of sin the self is "the center of everything and it is troublesome to others in that it seeks to make them subservient." To Luther pride and self-love are synonymous, both leading to what he called the "lust of the soul" in turning away from God to the creature. As between the holiness of God and the sinfulness of man, the difference is so radical, according to Christian orthodoxy, that man is convicted not of particular breaches but of being human and not divine.[1]

This radical discontinuity between God and man has its own perils, not the least of which is a person's indifference to everyday moral, social, and political concerns. Reinhold Niebuhr is bolder than most neoorthodox theologians in pointing out how religion degenerates into defeatism and despair toward things of the secular world when the religionist, on an asocial quest for the divine, withdraws from the close at hand because he thinks its claims have no significance in the sight of God. Niebuhr's many years of political and social involvement demonstrated a nonseparatist attitude. "Nevertheless," he wrote, "the tendency of religion to obscure the shades and shadows of moral life, by painting only the contrast between the white radiance of divine holiness and the darkness of the world, remains a permanent characteristic of the religious life."[2] The contrast identifies the two cities in Augustine's fifth-century *City of God*, and the two realms in Rudolf Otto's twentieth-century *The Idea of the Holy*. In its biblical context, the contrast identifies Babel, rising from the plains of Shinar (Gen. 11:1–19), and the new Jerusalem, "descending out of heaven from God" (Rev. 21:10). The contrast is nothing less than the beginning and the end, Genesis and Revelation. No mythicist's circle makes the two one; a linear definitiveness keeps the two two.

If indifference to the everyday world is one peril implicit in radical discontinuity, another is total engrossment with it and preoccupation with worldly accomplishments. The artist is especially susceptible to such centeredness. Again it is Isaiah which, in proclaiming the only real Creator, denounces the idol-makers who live deceived in their vain imaginings, taking pride in the things they have wrought and worshiping their art as totems of God (Isa. 45). To turn away from the ultimate source of creation to worship what their own hands had fashioned was not unlike the consummation reached in the Mephistophelian pact of the medieval legend. In this case, the covenant was made not with God but the devil. The aspiring mind turned from theology to black magic in order to gain forbidden knowledge, to know all things, and then to *create* a whole out of a fragmented world—to make all things new. The price of this demoniac involvement was expulsion from the paradise of love, from the ordinary communion with ordinary human beings. Analyzing Thomas Mann's Faustian theme, Erich Kahler suggests that the ecstasy of artistic creation arises from the agony of isolation. The mind "builds its own Heaven, and has to pay for it with its own Hell."[3] Medieval drama externalized the action, making religiously vivid the paradox between human aspiration in quest of adventure, beauty, power, wealth, truth, and, on the other hand, the soul's destruction brought about by its excessive appetites. One of the most provocative themes in Western culture, it appears in Marlowe, Goethe, Hawthorne, Mann, Valéry, and Sartre to name but a few notable writers. The Faustian figure is so pervasive, Kahler thinks, as to symbolize modern man, whose "frenzied pursuit of an arrogant technology . . . will turn out to have been a pact with the Devil."[4]

The point needs to be stressed that the Christian believer does not perceive the artist's position, in the last analysis, as being any more precarious than that of anyone else who overestimates his power and significance. As for artists, even Cal-

vin had celebrated the great gifts of intelligence and imagination that God had bestowed upon them. There was no
question that, endowed with a longing for truth and beauty,
people displayed impressive achievements in the arts as well
as in the sciences, philosophy, and law. Calvin recognized
that those whom scripture calls "natural men" were, indeed,
"sharp and penetrating." "Let us," he adjured, "learn by their
example how many gifts the Lord left to human nature even
after it was despoiled of its true good."[5] Furthermore, it is
well to remember that Calvin was a man of the Renaissance
before he was a Reformer. In his hands French prose took on
an exactness and strength that made it a vehicle for theological
writing of the highest order.[6]

Notwithstanding, there was also the incontrovertible fact
of pride and sin, although the Renaissance, according to T. E.
Hulme, eradicated the incontrovertibility of it and later
thinkers rejected the fact outright.[7] It might be said that in the
idea of "notwithstanding" the real significance of the Reformation lies. The discontinuity which the term implies was the
same that broke the medieval synthesis of nature and grace,
reason and revelation.[8] For notwithstanding all reasonable
evidence to the contrary, human nature *is* inclined toward the
achievements of self and away from those of the Almighty, a
theological principle so basic as to make evident the corollary,
namely, that art, originating from a self that is preoccupied
with its own expression, may be a *fleur du mal.*

The point is crucial in drawing distinctions between art and
religion. Critics and theologians in recent years have attempted to show how the one discipline elucidates the other.[9]
But this commendable effort has its dangers too. Is it correct,
for example, to regard the Bible as secular literature and then
examine St. Mark as a poet, or analyze the entire scripture as a
birth-death-rebirth archetype?[10] And is it legitimate, while
rejecting Calvin's ideas, to declare the *Institutes* as "one of the
great and liberating acts of imagination"?[11] On the other
hand, how legitimate is it for the theologian to call Picasso's
Guernica the greatest Protestant painting in the twentieth
century but say nothing about its aesthetics?[12] As T. S. Eliot

recognized when he questioned whether one needed to believe Dante's theology to believe his art, the problem concerns the context in which the critic or the theologian con-
ducts his respective work.[13] If the context is aesthetic, then
certain judgments about the Bible may turn out to be grossly
inadequate. The same danger threatens the theologian who
judges art within his theological definitions. Indeed, how can
there be meaningful distinctions or, for that matter, a meaningful union between art and theology, image and idea?

The American Puritans continue to shed light on this
timely issue, and the ideas of Jonathan Edwards best serve to
represent them. At the outset we need to remember that in
theological matters Edwards never separated sensibiity from
doctrine, heart from head. Were it only for his intellectualiz-
ing about religious experience he would not command the
attention he receives, nor would he merit this attention were
his religious feelings not only rigorously intellectual. Carica-
tures invariably overlook one side or the other, as they do
with Calvin. In Edwards's system there is an ever-present
inner connection, a congruence between the speculative and
the affectional. The affectional side includes imagination and
vision. Edwards not only joined sensibility and doctrine but,
like his Puritan forebearers, he also shaped doctrine according
to an underlying vision that rose from certain dictates of inspiration and certain great flashes of insight.

Students of Edwards have noted the characteristically aesthetic quality in his work. To cite only four: Samuel Perkins
Hayes, early in this century, called attention to Edwards's
combination of "searching irrefutable logic with a vivid orien-
tal imagination"; Joseph Haroutunian later argued that Edwards's view of man was persistently "intellectual and aesthetic"; Edwin H. Cady analyzed the "artistry" in Edwards's
famous Enfield sermon; and Roland Delattre devoted an
elaborate study to Edwards's aesthetics and theological ethics.[14]

In studying Edwards within this framework of aesthetics, it
is well-nigh irresistible to acclaim him a great poet, one who
stands separate from others and who, in E. M. W. Tillyard's

description of a poet, inhabits "heavens and hells unbearable by the ordinary man."[15] We can see such a person in the light that Shakespeare viewed Timon of Athens: "The middle of humanity thou never knewest, but the extremity of both ends" (*Timon of Athens*, 4.3. 300–1). It was not only Edwards's intellectual might but also his powerful imagination that enabled him to achieve the rare combination of clarity of thought and depth of insight. Moreover, this same combination brought vitality and concreteness to his sermons. Cast though they were in the form of cold logic, they were illumined by brilliant imagery and an underlying vision that can be called aesthetic. Finally, this imaginative range encompassed heights and depths of the human spirit known only to the greatest poetic visionaries.

In spite of these attributes, it is not enough to rest one's interpretation upon Edwards's aesthetic vision and to say he worked as an artist. For once again the distinction needs to be made between the aesthetic and the religious. For Edwards, the two are joined only when the spiritual regeneration of the artist unites them. Only when divine grace illumines the heart does the aesthetic vision become the religious. At the root of the matter is the inclination of the heart, whether toward self or God, and the motive that follows from the one or the other. Whichever the orientation, art is still art, but Edwards was not satisfied to stop at this level. Unless the heart's motive be taken into account, appraisals of human works must necessarily remain incomplete. The issue is not ultimately aesthetic but religious. In the light that the believer interprets as God's truth all works are seen as secondary and derivative; whereas outside the light, even though their nature has not changed, works falsely appear as ultimate because the self in the same darkness also appears this way. Open to the light, the artist creates to the glory of God; closed to it, he creates to his own glory.

From childhood Edwards was deeply moved by the world in which he lived; his *Personal Narrative* records the astonishing depth of feeling he achieved. He was especially moved by the sense of beauty and proportion, natural beauty being a "type" or emanation, however inadequate, of divine excellency. Still, there was something faintly detached and even impersonal about such a sense, something merely aesthetic, if religious experience were restricted to beauty alone. For Edwards the total religious vision depended not only upon apprehensions of divine beauty but, supremely, upon the revelation of Christ. Edwards's supreme passion, says Haroutunian, was the glory of God not in cosmic beauty alone but in "the face of Jesus Christ."[16] Beauty apart from the face remained too abstract, the vision too general. Only in and through the face—that is, Christ's love, humility, and saving grace—did true Christian vision obtain. This is to say that within the total meaning of life the aesthetic experience becomes the religious.[17] The total meaning for Edwards shone forth in the Incarnation. Christology was the touchstone of all knowledge. He affirmed that God does not exist in sublime isolation as the totality and essence of beauty but that he comes down to the level of man, reveals himself as man, and establishes a relationship with man, face to face. Nowhere else do the mercy and love of God appear so brightly, said Edwards, "as they do in the face of Jesus Christ."[18] The meaning of this statement depends upon regenerate vision. Such is the eye of faith by which Edwards preached and by which he expected to be understood, for neither natural imagination nor aesthetic vision could make understandable the distinction between a historical Jesus and a kerygmatic Christ.

In a similar way W. H. Auden stated that it is never solely through imagination that a person reconciles "the profane appearance and the sacred assertion" of the one who looked like any other man, yet claimed to be the Way, the Truth, and the Life. Likewise, it is impossible to behold Christ in aesthetic terms either on the stage or in visual arts. The best that a painter can do is to paint "either the Bambino with the Madonna or the dead Christ on the cross. . . . But neither a baby nor a corpse can say *I am the way*, etc."[19] In much the same way C. S. Lewis remarked that "the injunction to obey Christ has meaning: the injunction to obey Shakespeare is meaningless."[20] The issue goes beyond imagination and art to the spiritual realm of which Edwards spoke, to the capacity to reach divine truth as revealed through Christ in the everyday world that all people inhabit.

It needs repeating that the consciousness considered here is uniquely Christian and that such consciousness is unique. Admittedly, it makes sense only to an asserting faith that something has divine meaning or sacred character. Only as beheld from within the circle of faith does an object, for example, become sacramental; outside the faith it has no more importance than its secular worth ascribes to it.

For the American Puritans, Christian faith preceded the vision that eventuated in the word, whether as sermon or poem. To confuse this order was to misunderstand the relationship between religion and its artistic vessel. We might ask whether scripture is literary because it conforms to certain generic patterns, or whether the religious affections of witnessing writers in some way influenced these patterns. Is the biblical climax as presented in the marriage of Heaven and Earth an artistic or a religious achievement? Is the Incarnation something created by the human imagination, or is it something by which the imagination is vitalized? The philosopher George Santayana, a colleague of Josiah Royce at Harvard, postulated that the idea of Christ "had to be constructed by the imagination in response to [man's] moral demands." Accordingly, human imagination transforms the historical into the kerygmatic. Santayana thought the whole Christian doctrine is religious and efficacious "only when it becomes poetry" because only as poetry does doctrine become "a genuine expression of human life."[21]

Because of the power ascribed to the imagination the Puritans would have regarded this argument as insidious. Santayana attributed to human imagination the power to transform the secular into the sacred; Edwards and his theological brethren, on the contrary, believed that the sacred needs no human instrumentality. Religious orthodoxy held that redemptive power belongs to God and not to man and his art; that man transforms nothing except as he himself is transformed through the power of God; and that unless religious vision extends beyond the aesthetic, the artist will not reach the full extremities of reality, including those of divine beauty and excellency. Art will remain only art, sermons only sermons, words only human vessels, unless made transparent by what Edwards called the "spiritual opening of the eyes in conversion."[22] Only through regenerate eyes, so the argument goes, is it possible to see redemption as a Christian "epic" (Santayana), the Incarnation as a "gigantic metaphor" (Knight), and biblical history as a "mythological" drama (Kroner).[23] Whatever artistic qualities these terms signify, it is not through art but through Christ that the Christian event is transformed into epic, metaphor, and myth. The Puritans would have thought it absurd to suppose that the one-sided will of man through imagination could bring about the man-God event.

Certain of these ideas reverberate through C. S. Lewis' *Rehabilitation and Other Essays* (1939) in which he speculates, for example, that the Christian will find more hedonistic pleasure in literature than the cultured pagan will, who is apt to make a religion of his aesthetic experience and prepare for pleasure as if it were martyrdom. The Christian will enjoy literature as he does countless other things, knowing that he can play as well as eat to the glory of God. But like all other things of the world, literature remains secondary to the greater glory; it is adjectival to the greater noun.[24]

Like everyone else, the artist lives in relationship to the world around him. This relationship identifies him first as a human being before it recognizes him as an artist. As an artist taking great stock in originality, creativeness, genius, spontaneity, he may believe that these attributes set him apart and entitle him to privilege. Like M. H. Abrams's distinction between the mirror and the lamp,[25] the artist set apart from others is tempted to think of his mind as a microcosm illumined by the self-generating lamp of his imagination. To Lewis, however, the fact of relationship places the artist's supposed autonomy in a less grandiose position, one that presupposes not only a horizontal relationship to community but a vertical one to a sovereign truth. Such multiple relationships put an entirely different interpretation upon human originality, genius, and so on. No longer are these attributes seen as special to the artist alone, at least not in any separate ontological sense, but as attributes shared by others and reflecting a higher source. Existing not in his own microcosm but in what Abrams calls a "heterocosm" of relationships, the artist, then, may not be a light after all but a mirror reflecting the greater light. To Christian consciousness literature remains an adjectival thing to enjoy, study, ponder if worthy. But taken as evidence of the grandeur of human creatureliness, existing outside of relationship, it is a golden calf.

In Lewis's theological terms, to be outside of relationship is understood as alienation from being *(aversio a Deo)* and a turning to creatures *(conversio ad creaturam)*. It is a forgetting of being and an effort to establish life upon beings and their finite creations. To take art too seriously is to take the artist (and oneself) in the same way. The danger is to accord the artist a position which, as a human being, he does not merit. Artistic creativity does not excuse inhumanity, meanness of spirit, pride; nor do the artist's experiences and feelings as well as his art have transcendent value merely because they are his. Critical heroworshiping to the contrary, the artist inhabits no empyreal realm, and his imagination and genius do not make him one of the "elect." Of no ultimate significance is the fact that the Industry of Criticism canonizes literary works and exhumes each trashy word and petty acerbity of some author, as if his utterances were mystical truth.

Lewis's summary gets at the crux, and is worth quoting at length:

> I think there is so great a difference of temper that a man whose mind was at one with the mind of the New Testament would not, and indeed could not, fall into the language which most critics now adopt. In the New Testament the art of life itself is an art of imitation: can we, believing this, believe that literature, which must derive from real life, is to aim at being 'creative,' 'original,' and 'spontaneous'. 'Originality' in the New Testament is quite

plainly the prerogative of God alone; even within the triune being of God it seems to be confined to the Father. The duty and
happiness of every other being is placed in being derivative, in
reflecting like a mirror. Nothing could be more foreign to the
tone of scripture than the language of those who describe a saint
as a 'moral genius' or a 'spiritual genius' thus insinuating that his
virtue or spirituality is 'creative' or 'original'. If I have read the
New Testament aright, it leaves no room for 'creativeness' even
in a modified or metaphorical sense. Our whole destiny seems to
lie in the opposite direction, in being as little as possible ourselves, in acquiring a fragrance that is not our own but borrowed,
in becoming clean mirrors filled with the image of a face that is
not ours. I am not here supporting the doctrine of total depravity, and I do not say that the New Testament supports it; I am
saying only that the highest good of a creature must be crea-
turely—that is, derivative or reflective—good. In other words, as
St. Augustine makes plain (*De Civ. Dei*,xx, cap. I), pride does
not only go before a fall but is a fall—a fall of the creature's
attention from what is better, God, to what is worse, itself.[26]

The artist does not create or bring into existence beauty or
truth but simply captures in his art some reflection of the
same all-encompassing life in which he has his own being.
Lewis reminds his readers that the artist in the Homeric tradition was the "pensioner" of the muse; in the Platonic tradition he had affinities with a transcendent form partly imitable
on earth; in the Aristotlean tradition he saw his work in terms
of *mimesis,* or in the Augustan tradition as an imitation of
nature. What Lewis rejects is the Romantic theory of genius
sui generis: creativity as autonomous, independent, non-
derivative, and art as self-expression.
    Still another to cast a pale eye on the Romantic theory of
creativity is Howard Mumford Jones, who observed that the
Greek poets, content with a "profound lack of originality,"
accepted what was prescribed and adapted it to everyday life.
They depended upon an inherited ritual and subject matter,
and intended their art to serve a religious purpose, often to
propitiate the gods, to utter prayers, or to recite ceremonial
sayings. The function of art made unnecessary the compul-

sion on the part of the artist to invent new themes and styles. As for Christian art and its prescriptions, Byzantine rigidity did not diminish its artistic radiance, and the prescribed themes of Christianity satisfied "the humblest carpenter helping to produce the Noah's-ark play to the lofty genius of Dante." Even Chaucer "retells everything on authority," just as the medieval altarpiece "is never original," the book of hours is "a miracle of inherited pattern," and the Gothic cathedral is "a building in which tradition governs all."[27] In each case the individual artist was part of a tradition larger than his own private world. Standing within tradition including its circle of faith, he created works of art made meaningful as they reflected a creative spirit energized by the larger informing spirit.

What happens when the artist stands outside the normative circle; when his prophetic or ritualistic function disappears with the disappearance of the circle itself; when, in short, art becomes divorced from faith and myth? No longer depending upon tradition for his authority, the artist becomes his own authority by reducing everything to ego. Insights, experiences, and feelings take on ultimate value because they are his alone. What he comes to learn, however, is that independence is another form of alienation, and originality only hides despair. For all the terror darkening Puritan consciousness, it nevertheless was a terror responding to an irrefutable and hierarchical order. Regardless of its awful pronouncements, there was extending through it a slender, still unbroken thread of divine mercy. A far worse terror inheres in a world where "all men are just accumulations, dolls stuffed with sawdust swept up from the trash heaps where all previous dolls had been thrown away the sawdust flowing from what wound in what side that not for me died not."[28] William Faulkner's Quentin Compson would rather have been damned and consigned to hell, having a structured moral order thus confirmed, than to exist willy-nilly in a world where even love and sorrow are empty chambers of despair and art is only a momentary solace. This is the annihilating terror that destroys the Romantic soul whose consummation is its destruction. Holding to no radical otherness and affirming itself as the only great noun, the self collapses into an immense vacancy.

II

If one needs historical confirmation, the guns of August 1914 will obligingly sound again in modern memory. Paul Fussell's book is about the guns as ironic action, specifically about the Great War, which brought death to eight million after two human beings, the Archduke Francis Ferdinand and his consort, had been shot in Yugoslavia. This was indeed a great "theater of war" fought by conscripted armies whose members, temporarily taken out of "real life," were costumed in clothes they did not choose, given words they found difficult to memorize, and sent into battle amid the roses of Picardy and the poppies of Flanders—the war comprising what Fussell calls "patterns of farce and comedy [imposed] onto the blank horrors or meaningless vacancies of experience."[29] What could be more ironic, for example, than General Douglas Haig's letter to his wife written just prior to the battle of the Somme ("I feel that every step in my plan has been taken with the Divine help"), and then the count of 60,000 men killed or wounded on the very first day, 1 July 1916?[30] Perhaps surpassing even this irony is the sight of one British regiment showing its sporting spirit by dribbling a soccer ball toward German lines and then being mowed down by machine guns. If Fussell's book documents Wallace Stevens's ironic line, "How red the rose that is the soldier's wound," then Bruno Bettelheim's *The Informed Heart*, which analyzes the way the science of one race dehumanized another, or Elie Wiesel's *Night,* which re-creates the way the same race sought to blot out the other, makes the whole Romantic and meliorist philosophy a hideous embarrassment. The final fact of 70 million slaughtered in half a century corroborates Fussell's perception that "dawn has never recovered from what the Great War did to it."[31]

When Stephen Graham toured the Somme battlefields in

1920, he found that full daylight did not properly illuminate them. "Sunlight and noonday," he wrote, "do not always show us truth." They suggest too insistently things like vitality, ecstasy, and soaring Romantic consciousness. "Only in the grey light of afternoon and evening, and looking with the empty eye-socket of night-darkness can one easily apprehend what is spread out here—the last landscape of tens of thousands who lie dead."[32] The realization that dawn or noonday will never tell the full story indicates that Thoreau's morning star or John Muir's range of light, Hester Prynne's flood of sunshine or Per Hansa's mighty kingdom, remain but incomplete visions. We are legatees of both the Western frontier and the terrible Western front.

Despite the echoing memories, humanist critics in the 1920s steadfastly attempted to uphold the old verities, if not of Romanticism per se then of human dignity and reason. Irving Babbitt and Paul Elmer More waged their own battles against the literary naturalism of Theodore Dreiser, Eugene O'Neill, John Dos Passos, and Sinclair Lewis, who depicted human behavior in terms of glandular and environmental determinism. What Babbitt and his disciples, including More, strove to maintain was a sense of proportion, poise, control, reason, moral will—in short, what Babbitt called in *Humanism and America,* the "law of measure." Not only was this law of measure his criterion for judging literature but it was also the noblest of ethical norms. His search for a model in literature and life rested on this ideal, one that he believed must be preserved in the face of historical events and scientific forces diminishing humans to little more than pawns on a darkling stage or biological and psychological organisms.

Norman Foerster added his voice to the embattled humanists. Even while he paid tribute to the New Critics— specifically T. S. Eliot, William Empson, John Crowe Ransom, Allen Tate, Cleanth Brooks, and R. P. Blackmur—for their close reading of literary texts and their sensitive discriminations, Foerster demanded more from criticism than formalist analysis. Writing in the 1940s when the lights of Europe and the world were going out again, he urged literary critics to explain literature for its wisdom about human dignity and worth. If, he said, critics have no concern for these humanistic values, they "might as well close up shop and let the tempest ride."[33]

Still another humanist critic to take up arms was Douglas Bush, who believed that the reason we read literature at all is that literature is ethical, "it makes us better." "Unless literature is in its effect didactic," he said, "I do not know any sufficient reason for its existence."[34] Bush regarded the literary critic as a moralist, as one who appraises literature for what it shows about human life in its full moral range. To the ancients and the Renaissance writers literature served a didactic function; it was, Bush said, "philosophy teaching by example"; it moved men "to the love and practice of virtue and the abhorence of vice."[35] The aim of literature was identical with that of education, namely, virtuous action. Like Foerster, Babbitt, and humanist critics back to Matthew Arnold, he wanted to direct literary criticism toward the recognition of this moral end. He thought of literature as saving human beings from their craving egos and barbarous ways. Both Foerster in the 1940s and Bush in the 1960s had a sense of urgency. At a time when science, politics, and technology, including the most awesome kinds of weaponry, appeared to threaten the physical and spiritual survival of everyone, these humanist critics envisioned an eschatological need for mankind to regain a sense of moral balance, taste, and imagination. Specifically, Bush found in Christian humanism a sanity, a strength, and an imaginative vision that contributed to the greatness of Renaissance literature and that he thought still must serve as a literary touchstone. He held that a certain interaction of classical and Christian ideals allowed the Renaissance writers to view man as heroically living amid forces of good and evil, and as reaching heights and depths of beingness all but extinguished in what he considered the present dehumanized age of modern determinism. At the heart of the matter for Bush and the others was a theory of criticism demanding a philosophy of man. Without such a groundwork the critic presumably would suffer disorientation and an absence of critical standards.

The truth of the matter was that such traditionalism, which the earlier humanists sought to uphold, was all but dead. Nietzsche's announcement concerning the death of God applied ominously to civilization, a fact accounting for the pervasive theme of death in modern literature. R. W. B. Lewis observes that "twentieth century literature began on the note of death."[36] His reference is to James Joyce's opening lines of *Dubliners,* but Lewis also points out that disease, decay, paralysis, and death pervade both theme and tone in Mann, Woolf, Forster, Proust, and Camus. If indeed a great malaise, a sense of loss, a spiritual death characterize our late twentieth-century culture, the question needs to be asked whether humanism as a concept can survive in this malignant air. Lewis finds hope in what he calls the "picaresque saint" who struggles to hold in balance the nightmarish facts of contemporary life and the "vital aspiration" to transcend them.

The term "existential" serves as an all-inclusive rubric to describe what is left of the humanist's posture. Difficult to define, the term grants the human only his mortal existence, characterized by absurdity, alienation, anxiety, and despair. All the best laid plans, all the previous consciousness of power, independence, and importance fade away, and he is left abandoned in an indifferent universe with only his existence to affirm. He is permitted no pipe dreams. Alongside this existential man, the traditional humanist with his inherited values appears sadly incongruous. When depicted in modern fiction, he is Roquentin, the self-taught man in Sartre's *Nausea,* and Mr. Ramsey in Woolf's *To the Lighthouse.*

Readers today find it necessary to take up their Kierkegaard, Heidegger, and Unamuno to understand the century's representative characters like Beckett's Vladimir and Estragon, Conrad's Kurtz, Eliot's Prufrock, Bellow's Herzog, and countless others who in one way or another dramatize the apparent irrelevance of humanistic assumptions about civilized man. And what do critics do when confronting these fictional protagonists who, appearing fragmented beyond hope, have lost their identity in an advanced stage of entropy? The contemporary humanist has witnessed his values disappear in whatever is his equivalent to the endless rows of white crosses at Verdun, the ovens of Dachau, the mushroom cloud over Hiroshima, and the boil of orange napalm in Vietnam. He has traveled the road to hell and, like Kurtz, has heard his heart beat in unison with the murderers'. What moral insights does a humanist bring to nightmares and ashcans? What does humanism say about spectral man? This is the problem Wylie Sypher addresses in his penetrating study, *Loss of the Self in Modern Literature and Art.* Given the all but unrecognizable quality of self in modern man, Sypher questions whether humanism can remain viable. But affirming a residual of "post-existential humanism," he thinks that however far man has traveled toward entropic darkness, he still cannot alienate himself from his own state of consciousness. Man still has an existence which he is not able to diminish "below a certain point."[37] A surviving humanism grants this minimal self. For all its banal evil and shapeless anonymity, the self still endures. Named Mal or Lok or Liku or Fa—the Neanderthal names William Golding gives his characters in *The Inheritors*—he still exists to ask himself, "Who am I?"

One reason Sypher's concept of minimum consciousness must be taken seriously is that it applies first of all to the artist and his existential involvement in what he writes. The claim has to do with intentionality. Many critics have set aside this issue, heeding the supposed warning of W. K. Wimsatt and Monroe G. Beardsley against committing the so-called intentional fallacy. In general these formalist critics have acquiesced in the privileged standpoint and the ontological hierarchy that Wimsatt and Beardsley accord the artist and his work. The widely accepted argument for discounting intention as integral to art is of course that either the poet succeeded in doing what he intended, in which case we have the successful poem, or else he failed. In either case, to inquire about intention takes the critic "outside" the poem, another way of saying that such inquiry takes him dangerously close to the artist's consciousness. According to Wimsatt and Beardsley, the critic needs to demand only that the poem as artifice "works." The poem simply *is;* it is "a feat of style"— autonomous, public, objective.[38] The underlying assumption is that literature bears testimony to some kind of autonomous activity of the mind, some distinctive and privileged way of being in the world to be understood in terms of its own heuristic purposes.

Left out of account is the artist's struggle for meaning and the fact that his words bear testimony to this struggle. In the post-World War II years, a new humanism has emerged that recognizes, in answer to barren formalism, that the critical enterprise requires the interpretation of consciousness, be it only minimal consciousness. Accordingly, certain French critics, like Marcel Raymond, Albert Béguin, and Georges Poulet, have rejected the notion that a "literary" consciousness is in any way a privileged one and that its language transcends the confusion and duplicity inherent in the everyday use of language.[39] That formalism failed to take into account the rag-and-bone consciousness actualized in language leads Paul de Man to forsake what he calls "the barren world of ontological reduction" and to affirm "the wealth of lived experience," including the suffering and joy implicit in intentionality.[40] This perspective holds that the *beingness* of the artist precedes that of his art. His quest for meaning and self is seen as giving literary consciousness and language their true reality. This is the struggle that Lionel Trilling has called "the sentiment of being," unifying intention and structure.[41] Far from threatening the unity of art, the struggle for being-ness, which is inseparable from intentionality, establishes this unity. In this way language is redeemed from its hierarchical separateness, it is humanized; and the artist's consciousness is incarnated in his word.

In actuality it may be asked whether the completeness of a literary form implies a corresponding totality of the constitutive self. On the one hand, Paul de Man thinks that the human center, always hidden and out of reach, will never be found. What happens at best when consciousness is heightened is the feeling of fragility, discontinuousness, contingency, temporality. The literary form, far from an unchanging and eternal object, necessarily decays with imprecision because it partakes of the human consciousness that created it. Trilling, on the other hand, argues that the sentiment of being is "the sentiment of being strong," a self-defining energy of self contriving that its "center shall hold, that the circumference of the self keep unbroken, that the person be an integer, impenetrable, perdurable, and autonomous in being if not in action."[42] Whether one can forge a self in the smithy of art or whether such coalescence is made impossible by its own temporality, the central issue remains that of consciousness. In emphasizing this issue, Geoffrey H. Hartman says that the "*I am* implicit in every act of consciousness is also the *I am* revealed by art. In art as elsewhere, consciousness feels out or I-am-izes the world."[43] In other words, this subjective component in art abrogates the authority of creative or critical privilege.

Consciousness can be interpreted as a shaping or structural power. Coleridge made clear that this power is intentional. Unlike natural phenomena in which a tree, for example, is itself by an act not its own, human imagination empowers a person to shape that which he will become. Consciousness, intentionality, imagination—all relate to the humanist's structure of self and art. We ask, however, whether consciousness is too vast for control. Can imagination fix the flux of consciousness? This question concerns the artistic process, the grasping and fixing of reality and the structuring of that which is significant in human experience. From earliest time the artist's consciousness has compelled him to find geometric forms to symbolize feelings, then to give these forms balance, coherence, and symmetry; to construct a system of relationships; to bring the world into order, into word or image, for the sake of the identity and the very survival of consciousness itself.

But with the Romantics we have seen consciousness either

expand beyond form or break down completely. The earlier hope was that Romanticism could capture the conception or idea of form and embody it. That we could thus participate in the ideal turned out instead to be a denial of self in the contingent world of being. With the bankruptcy of idealism we have witnessed the fragmenting of consciousness, such that in our limitations we cannot participate in what we imagine nor can we integrate what we conceive. Our recourse often is to disown our feelings, domesticate them, or reject them. Seemingly unable to shape satisfactory constructs, we swirl in the midst of our vertiginous, dreamlike condition, content to have artists reveal consciousness in its primitive vitality and yet also troubled by the fact that they cannot bring order to this energy.

The question is whether order and symmetry in art reflect a corresponding self. Romanticism shattered this equation by reaching too far, by seeking infinitude through the lamp of imagination and then trusting language to bear the burden of the vision. The outcome testified to human finitude and the breakdown of conventional form. The New Critics chose to set aside speculation about the former, turning instead to aesthetic matters and believing that some kind of rebuilt artistic organicism could obviate the malaise and confusion of modern consciousness. The danger they risked was in making art nonreferential, a dead end, its own ontology, and to lose sight of what Murray Krieger has called the Manichean quality inherent in art. Krieger believes that instead of being merely nonreferential, art also must be referential; it is both a closed world of meaning and a window through which we see the outside world. The dilemma is between artistic organicism and the existential world outside. To resolve this dilemma Krieger thinks the critic needs to find not only an order doing justice to the inner complexity of the artistic work, but also a moral order, a metaphysic, a theodicy that will do justice to the fearful paradoxes of experiences. He calls for a mythical and religious dimension (a "thematic") to undergird both art and criticism.[44]

This notion raises the further question of whether so-called aesthetic order by itself is anything else than the illusion of art and the vanity of imagination. For all the complexities that vain imaginings seek to fix, perhaps the essence of art is only in the illusion that these complexities are held together and shaped into aesthetic unity. Thus we talk about the tensions that give art its dynamics. Yet if art succeeds in fixing the ambiguities, it paradoxically has failed in another dimension; for if it brings order to the raw materials of life, it has nullified their power. James Guetti argues that the real motive of metaphor is the "expectation" of order that can never be fulfilled or satisfied. Imagination as a shaping function necessarily implies its own failure. The illusion of coherency, which is art, cannot be preserved when coherency is itself sought, for the illusion contradicts its raw vitality.[45]

In other words art has to do with the existential *quest* for order as much as with the achieved aesthetic order. Such a quest is necessarily a "quest for failure," as Walter J. Slatoff has described Faulkner's "failure."[46] The point recognizes that aesthetic order as a privileged and hierarchical ontology is an artifice, a mere play. If the play is elevated to human ultimacy, religious consciousness condemns it as vanity. When Guetti describes the essential hollowness of "as if" thinking as the "process of continually and self-hypnotically reconstructing the illusion of order," he is calling attention to the folly of expecting art to accomplish more than it can. The artifice breaks down the moment its language opens to an anterior and posterior reality. The cold pastoral dissolves into the real confusion whence it came.

Bereft of the old verities and yet unwilling to settle for the game of "as if," today's humanists find themselves with little that can serve as a starting point except it be existence itself. That the struggle for meaning precedes and infuses art may be difficult to affirm if consciousness is seen as coextensive with nihilism and if our modern paradigm is truly the weightlessness that finds us thrown into existence and left homeless amid the random flow of contingent and absurd details. Even so, the risk of struggling has a truer ring of honesty than does the formalist's game. Furthermore, it provides an alternative

for the person searching through the rubble of Western culture for something restorative.

Affirming consciousness affords a way into the psychic
forces that bind us all together. Deeper than objective history
with its restrictive view of man as only a social and political
animal, the consciousness remaining for the humanist to
affirm leads to something greater than community, something
that is not of men and least of all man-made; something toward which a person in the deeper part of himself can never
be alien and from which he will realize true community. It is a
consciousness bringing separate and alien selves into common
being. C. G. Jung described this vast and diffused coherence
as that which binds individuals among themselves to a race
and unites them with peoples of the past and their psychology.[47] Within these deeper levels of existence resides the
power of myth, which communities have found immemo-
rially wonderful, terrible, awesome, ungraspable, and sus-
taining. Myth appropriates this power; it speaks of the unknown in the cosmos, the community, and the self. From this
archaic energy in our nature we can identify with those images of antiquity which, as humanist William Barrett says,
"come down to us eyeless and lidless, eroded and scarred and
pocked by weather, and in that form they respose in the
pantheon of our imagination, not diminished but possibly
gaining a haunting power in their ruined state."[48] It is at this
level of consciousness, according to myth critic Maud Bodkin, that we pass from death to life "because we love the
brethren."[49] The point once again concerns the minimal consciousness of which Sypher speaks, and the restorative power
of myth that sustains life beyond the closed world of nihilism.

Despite what a social critic like Georg Lukács might see as
the danger of setting literature above or over and against the
world of historical experience, the greater danger is to restrict
literature to historicity.[50] When ecumenical authority comes
only from within a historical framework, and when human
consciousness knows no other dimension, then what we call
patterns of history become, like those of art, autonomous
illusions of coherency testifying to their own "failure." When

no authority exists beyond history, history itself becomes an artifice, which is another way of saying that unless history (and art) is seen as touching something beyond itself, it is nothing more than the hollow game of "as if" devoid of linked analogies and inexorably nihilistic. Thus culture itself disintegrates, proving that Freud was right when he observed that confused and helpless people will come to hate culture. To this we can add that, with no reference beyond themselves and no sources of power other than their man-made dynamo or reactor to hold things together, people will find their real action only in technology or, more immediately, in the narcissistic cult of personality.

But even this is not without its myth, and old Tiresias will not be deceived. Like him we have "walked among the lowest of the dead." We have seen that death has undone so many because the many have forsaken myth and religion. Eliot's *The Waste Land* is an obituary to the mythless man; it is itself the age-old myth of death, set in a country in which the inhabitants are spiritually dead and sexually sterile, a land wherein the very welfare of the king and the fecundity of the earth depend upon the ability of the people to ask the right questions about themselves and to act upon the dark encroachment that impels their questions. Literature finds its power in this same dark kingdom, not of death but of that collective experience of death known to all people regardless of time and culture. Likewise, literature finds its power in the collective experience of life, again beyond time and history.

Myth bespeaks a cycle of creation arising from destruction, birth growing out of death, and a symbolic community of things passing away in the unity of an infinite process. Of this mythical process even minmal human consciousness is not entirely bereft.

What brings artist and reader together is the consciousness of this process and their mutual submergence into the depths. In such consciousness are to be found the mysteries of community comprising the stuff of myth and nullifying the terror of nihilism. Consciousness of the primal, primordial, primitive source of art allows the poet no privileged exclusiveness.

The same applies to the humanist, for whom the meaning of art does not reside in the object alone nor in its historicity but in his own participation. The humanist's recourse is to enter the same mythic regions in order to understand the consciousness and intention of the artist and the sources of his art. The humanist critic is called to a shared humanness. His language, like that of the artist, constitutes his humanity and will be the means through which he communicates it. His existence is authenticated in his language. As Paul de Man again puts it, criticism thus becomes a matter of "hermeneutic circularity" wherein the critic unites with the artist as in an act of grace. For the humanist it is the only position he has left. It may be the best one he has ever had.

III

Yet the story is not fully told, not for a Christian consciousness that finds no rest even amid the reassurances of mythic existence. Granted that marvelous wonders occur when, as perceived by mythic consciousness, history's debris is swallowed up into cosmic totality and the sacredness of nature is restored. A person unified with the cosmic whole is open to receive cosmic hierophanies: physical nature incarnates and manifests the sacred and becomes a symbolic language, understandable to the interpreter standing in harmonious relationship. He reads nature as a prereflective, primitive, pagan language. Joined in community, alive to and linked with the sacred world, and quickened to the language of symbol and myth, he is reborn not into perfection but into totality. Nevertheless, something in all this still leaves Christian consciousness restless.

Mircea Eliade would have it the other way around: Christianity leaves mythic consciousness restless and disturbed. Whenever Christianity is less than "cosmic," a restriction Eliade thinks endemic, Christianity is at fault, for in emphasizing personal religious experience it leaves nature "desacralized." It empties nature of its gods or transforms them into devils. Through the centuries it "has emptied the cosmos of the sacred, and thus neutralized and banalized it."[51] A desacralized cosmos, devoid of theophanies and bereft of a sacred language, is mere substance to be studied, controlled, used, destroyed, but not to be "read" or assimilated. According to Eliade, Christianity severed man from nature, and nature from its gods, in order to make exclusive man's relationship with a single Godhead. Prior to the Judeo-Christian tradition the entire cosmos, including nature and man, was a harmonious whole, a sacred reality; but after the Hebrews replaced the Canaanite fertility gods with a singular Yahweh and the Christians embodied him in a singular person, nature as such fell way. Alienated from nature, human beings were seen as fallen and unredeemed, the legacy, according to Eliade, left by the Judeo-Christian religion.

Eliade's argument is powerful and age-old. What makes it compelling anew is his conviction like that of Wylie Sypher, that modern man, even though living in a fragmented and desacralized world, has not lost completely his minimal religious consciousness. Even though he is radically secularized and believes himself atheist, areligious, or, at least, indifferent, he is wrong because "he has not yet succeeded in abolishing the *homo religiosus* that is in him: he has only done away with (if he ever was) the *christianus*." In short, modern man "is left with being 'pagan,' without knowing it." He is minimally conscious of a world not completely one-dimensional, not completely devoid or emptied of spiritual reality. This minimal, mythic consciousness keeps him human, since a completely secularized life contradicts the definition of human life. An areligious society "does not yet exist"; in fact, "it *cannot exist* . . . [and] if it were achieved, it would perish after a few generations from boredom, from neurasthenia, or by collective suicide."[52] *Homo religiosus* retains his human identity by the fact that he yearns for a greater wholeness than mere ego supplies, a wholeness to be fully restored when reconciled with nature, sacralized, and then affirmed in mythic consciousness.

From time immemorial mythic consciousness has responded to an authoritative spiritual presence in and beyond

nature that establishes order and meaning to human life and
elevates it to a condition of relationship. Yet the question
intrudes whether being is fulfilled when nature and man are
reconciled into timeless unity; or whether it is somehow
fulfilled in the profound paradox that nothing worth doing
can be achieved in our lifetime, that nothing that is true or
beautiful or good makes complete sense in any immediate
context of history, that nothing we do, however virtuous, can
be accomplished alone—and, therefore, that we are restored
only by hope, faith, and love. The question pertains to the
difference between the consciousness of *homo religiosus* and
that of *christianus religiosus,* the one interpreted by a Mircea
Eliade and the other by a Reinhold Neibuhr.[53]

To speak of human consciousness presupposes a variegated
context that includes well-being in one instance and sickness
unto death in another. The ineluctable fact that humanness is
the foundation of all consciousness insures a context as multifarious as human life itself. Claims upon consciousness extend from rationality to madness, serenity to despair, joy to
woe, love to hate. Surpassing even these extremes is, on the
one hand, the consciousness of death as an abstract component in a philosophical system and, on the other, the consciousness of one's own impending death. A threat to personal existence shatters cosmic harmony in an instant. To
think of human consciousness as able to reconcile disparities
in some ideal process may do little to quiet the private dread
of one in whose deepest circuitry the best-laid connections
snap apart.

Brokenness is not the result of Christianity, as Eliade asserts, but a truth validated by it. Some thinkers have described this truth as that of tragic injustice: the disparity between what a person reasons should happen and what does
happen, the reversal undermining his sense of authority.
Others have defined it as heroic failure. Christian consciousness sees it as the tragedy of divine intervention that condemns even the person of goodwill who rests satisfied in
humanistic values and mythical consciousness—and also the
tragedy of human intervention that leaves crucified the person

who tries to live in one world according to the divine imperatives of another. Such consciousness of judgment suffers both
the knowledge of brokenness and the futility in attempting to
disguise it. Its heaven-bent "Why?" brings ambiguous answers. Friends one seeks for consolation, sleep. A thousand
times worse than physical pain or death, the true passion is
the agonizing sense of loss of one's own value.

Spanning the two centuries between Jonathan Edwards and
T. S. Eliot is a link that never bridged the fifty years between
the older Edwards and the younger Emerson. The link is that
of a Christian consciousness that, in Christ, lives in the sear-
ing knowledge of a shared suffering, and the faith of a shared
transfiguration: life lived in One who took the inward agony
and made of it, through love, eternal life.

> Who then devised the torment? Love.
> Love is the unfamiliar Name
> Behind the hands that wove
> The intolerable shirt of flame
> Which human power cannot remove.
>
> ("Little Gidding," iv)

Notes

Chapter 1

1. William Bradford, *Of Plymouth Plantation, 1620–1647*, ed. Samuel Eliot Morison (New York: Alfred A. Knopf, 1953), pp. 62, 61.

2. John Winthrop, "A Model of Christian Charity," in *Colonial American Writing*, 2d ed., ed. Roy Harvey Pearce (New York: Holt, Rinehart and Winston, 1969), p. 128. Italics mine.

3. John Cotton, "God's Promise to His Plantation," ibid., p. 68.

4. Vernon Louis Parrington, *Main Currents in American Thought* (New York: Harcourt, Brace, 1926), 1:109, 116.

5. Sacvan Bercovitch, ed., *The American Puritan Imagination: Essays in Revaluation* (London: Cambridge University Press, 1974), pp. 8–12; *The Puritan Origins of the American Self* (New Haven, Conn.: Yale University Press, 1975), pp. 132–34.

6. Ibid., pp. 165, 186.

7. Charles Feidelson, Jr., *Symbolism and American Literature* (Chicago: University of Chicago Press, 1953), pp. 88, 94, 89.

8. Perry Miller, "From Edwards to Emerson," in *Errand into the Wilderness* (New York: Harper and Row, 1964), pp. 195–96.

9. Feidelson, *Symbolism and American Literature*, p. 99.

10. Parrington, *Main Currents in American Thought*, 1:158.

11. Mason I. Lowance, Jr., "'Images or Shadows of Divine Things' in the Thought of Jonathan Edwards," in *Typology and Early American Literature*, ed. Sacvan Bercovitch (Amherst: University of Massachusetts Press, 1972), p. 241.

12. Samuel Mather, *Figures or Types of the Old Testament* 1683; reprint ed., New York: Johnson Reprint, 1969), p. 55.

13. Jonathan Edwards, *Works*, ed. Edward Hickman (London: F. Westley and A. H. Davis, 1834), 1:xiii.

14. Perry Miller, introduction to Jonathan Edwards, *Images and Shadows of Divine Things* (New Haven, Conn.: Yale University Press, 1948), p. 32.

15. Edwards, "A Dissertation Concerning the End for Which God Created the World," *Works*, 1:120. Edwards's italics.

16. Edwin H. Cady, "The Artistry of Jonathan Edwards," *New England Quarterly* 22 (March 1949):61–72

17. John Griffith, "Jonathan Edwards as a Literary Artist," *Criticism* 15 (Spring 1973):156–73. See also Annette Kolodny, "Imagery in the Sermons of Jonathan Edwards," *Early American Literature* 13 (Fall 1972):172–82.

18. Jonathan Edwards, "Miscellanies," in *The Philosophy of Jonathan Edwards from His Private Notebooks,* ed. Harvey G. Townsend (Eugene: University of Oregon Press, 1955), p. 115.

19. Edwards, in Perry Miller, "Jonathan Edwards on the Sense of the Heart," *Harvard Theological Review* 41 (April 1948):142. The major portion of this article consists of an excerpt from Edwards's "Miscellanies" (Item 782).

20. "The distribution [Edwards wrote] of human knowledge into speculative and sensible . . . indeed may be extended to all the knowledge we have of all objects whatsoever. . . . So that perhaps this distinction of the kinds of our knowledge into speculative and sensible, if duly weighed, will be found the most important of all" ("Miscellanies," p. 120).

21. Edwards's "Of the Prejudices of the Imagination" is included in Leon Howard, *"The Mind" of Jonathan Edwards: A Reconstructed Text* (Berkeley: University of California Press, 1963), pp. 146–48. Edwards's reference to the rationalists appears on p. 147; Howard's terms appear on p. 133.

22. John Locke, *An Essay Concerning Human Understanding* (London: G. Offor et al., 1819), 2:xxiii, 35.

23. Ernest Lee Tuveson, *The Imagination as a Means of Grace: Locke and the Aesthetics of Romanticism* (Berkeley: University of California Press, 1960), p. 97.

24. Jonathan Edwards, "Distinguishing Marks, " in *The Great Awakening,* ed. C. C. Goen (New Haven, Conn.: Yale University Press, 1972), p. 236.

25. Jonathan Edwards, *Treatise Concerning Religious Affections,* ed. John E. Smith (New Haven, Conn.: Yale University Press, 1959), p. 289n.

26. Jonathan Edwards, "The Future Punishment of the Wicked Unavoidable and Intolerable," in *Works,* 2:81; also in *Jonathan Edwards: Representative Selections,* rev. ed., eds. Clarence H. Faust and Thomas H. Johnson (New York: Hill and Wang, 1962), p. 146.

27. Edwards, *Religious Affections,* pp. 173–74.

28. Edwards, "Some Thoughts," in *The Great Awakening,* p. 436.

29. Edwards, *Religious Affections,* pp. 206–7.

30. Ibid., p. 274.

31. Ibid., p. 291.

32. H. Richard Niebuhr, *The Meaning of Revelation* (New York: Macmillan, 1941), p. 101.

33. Edwards, "Observations Concerning Faith," in *Works,* 2:580.

34. Edwards, *Religious Affections,* p. 274.

35. Edwards, "Miscellanies," p. 111.

36. Richard Kroner, *The Religious Function of Imagination* (New Haven, Conn.: Yale University Press, 1941), p. 37.

37. Edwards, "Some Thoughts," pp. 436–37.

38. Jonathan Edwards, *Images or Shadows of Divine Things,* ed. Perry Miller (New Haven, Conn.: Yale University Press, 1948). See Miller's introduction, pp. 1–41.

39. Edwards, *Religious Affections*, pp. 273, 275, 282–83.
40. Sören Kierkegaard, *Concluding Unscientific Postscript*, trans. David F. Swenson (Princeton, N.J.: Princeton University Press, 1941), pp. 347–48.
41. Edwards, *Religious Affections*, p. 274.
42. Ibid., p. 273.

Chapter 2

1. Sacvan Bercovitch, ed., *The American Puritan Imagination: Essays in Revaluation* (London: Cambridge University Press, 1974), pp. 3–8.
2. Sacvan Bercovitch, *The Puritan Origins of the American Self* (New Haven, Conn.: Yale University Press, 1975), pp. 136, 132–133, 184.
3. Perry Miller, *The New England Mind: The Seventeenth Century* (Cambridge, Mass.: Harvard University Press, 1963), p. 362.
4. M. H. Abrams, *Natural Supernaturalism: Tradition and Revolution in Romantic Literature* (New York: W. W. Norton, 1971), pp. 95, 29.
5. Jonathan Edwards, *The Nature of True Virtue*, ed. William K. Frankena (Ann Arbor: University of Michigan Press, 1960), p. 25.
6. Johann Fichte, *Addresses to the German Nation*, trans. R. F. Jones and G. H. Turnbull (Chicago and London: Open Court Publishing Co., 1922), p. 156.
7. Yvor Winters, "Maule's Curse," in *In Defense of Reason* (Denver, Colo.: Alan Swallow, n.d.), p. 170; F. O. Matthiessen, *American Renaissance: Art and Expression in the Age of Emerson and Whitman* (New York: Oxford University Press, 1941), p. 276; Richard Harter Fogle, *Hawthorne's Fiction: The Light and the Dark* (Norman: University of Oklahoma Press, 1964), p. 11; Hyatt H. Waggoner, "Art and Belief," in *Hawthorne Centenary Essays*, ed. Roy Harvey Pearce (Columbus: Ohio State University Press, 1964), p. 192.
8. Ursula Brumm, *American Thought and Religious Typology*, trans. John Hoaglund (New Brunswick, N.J.: Rutgers University Press, 1970), pp. 159, 161.
9. Marjorie J. Elder, *Nathaniel Hawthorne: Transcendental Symbolist* (Athens: Ohio University Press, 1969), pp. 171, 142.
10. Millicent Bell, *Hawthorne's View of the Artist* (Albany: State University of New York Press, 1962), p. 38.
11. Quoted in Mark Van Doren, *Nathaniel Hawthorne* (New York: William Sloane Associates, 1949), p. 24.
12. Quoted in Matthiessen, *American Renaissance*, p. 227.
13. Jay Leyda, *The Melville Log* (New York: Gordian Press, 1969), 1:381.
14. Matthiessen, *American Renaissance*, p. 225.
15. Leyda, *The Melville Log*, 2:674.
16. Quotations from Hawthorne's short stories come from *The Complete Works of Nathaniel Hawthorne*, 12 vols. (Boston: Houghton Mifflin, 1890).
17. Jonathan Edwards, *Original Sin*, ed. Clyde A. Holbrook (New Haven, Conn.: Yale University Press, 1970), p. 124. Edwards's italics.
18. Jonathan Edwards, *Treatise on Grace and Other Posthumously Published Writings*, ed. Paul Helm (Cambridge and London: James Clarke, 1971), pp. 30–33.
19. See M. H. Abrams, *The Mirror and the Lamp: Romantic Theory and the*

184   Radical Discontinuities

Critical Tradition (New York: Oxford University Press, 1953); also Matthiessen, *American Renaissance,* pp. 253–64.

20. Leyda, *The Melville Log,* 1:410.

21. Ibid.

22. Ibid., 1:380.

23. Ibid., 1:381.

24. Herman Melville, "Hawthorne and His Mosses," *The Literary World* (17 and 24 August 1850); reprinted in Leslie Fiedler, ed., *The Art of the Essay* (New York: Thomas Y. Crowell, 1958), p. 575.

25. James M. Cox, "The Scarlet Letter: Through the Old Manse and the Custom House," *Virginia Quarterly Review* 51 (Summer 1975):447.

26. Jonathan Edwards, "Men Naturally Are God's Enemies," *The Works,* ed. Edward Hickman (London: F. Westley and A. H. Davis, 1834), 2:134; John Calvin, *Institutes of the Christian Religion,* ed. John T. McNeill (Philadelphia: Westminster Press, 1960), 1:35.

27. Thomas Hooker, "A True Sight of Sin," in *The Puritans,* eds. Perry Miller and Thomas H. Johnson (New York: Harper and Row, 1963), 1:292.

28. References to *The Scarlet Letter* are to the Rinehart Edition (New York, 1947), introduction by Austin Warren. Chapter numbers are indicated in parentheses.

29. Erik H. Erikson, *Young Man Luther: A Study in Psychoanalysis and History* (New York: W. W. Norton, 1962), pp. 251–52.

30. Ibid., p. 251.

31. Rudolf Otto, *The Idea of the Holy,* trans. John W. Harvey, 2d ed. (London, Oxford University Press, 1950), p. 15.

32. Editor John T. McNeill notes that hell, in whatever physical metaphors it is depicted, is, for Calvin, essentially alienation (Calvin, *Institutes,* vol. 2, p. 1008n). See also John Milton, *Paradise Lost,* 5:877, specifically Abdiel's address to Satan: "O alienate from God, O spirit accurst." The Reformers' view of natural man's self-sufficiency is treated in William Pauck, *The Heritage of the Reformation* (Boston: Beacon Press, 1950), p. 9.

33. Paul Tillich, *The Protestant Era,* abridged ed., trans. James Luther Adams (Chicago: University of Chicago Press, 1957), p. xvi.

Chapter 3

1. R. W. B. Lewis, *The American Adam: Innocence, Tragedy, and Tradition in the Nineteenth Century* (Chicago: University of Chicago Press, 1955), p. 23.

2. Ibid., p. 22. Lewis's italics.

3. Johan Bojer, *The Great Hunger,* trans. W. J. Alexander Worster and C. Archer (New York: Grosset, 1919), p. 321.

4. O. E. Rölvaag, *The Boat of Longing,* trans. Nora Solum (New York: Harper and Brothers, 1933), p. 1.

5. O. E. Rölvaag, *The Third Life of Per Smevik,* trans. Ella Valborg Tweet and Solveig Zempel (Minneapolis, Minn.: Dillon Press, 1971), p. 4; originally entitled *Amerika-Breve (Letters from America,* 1912).

6. Ibid., pp. 11, 15.

7. John Heitmann, "Ole Edvart Rölvaag," *Norwegian-American Studies and Records,* 12 (1941):144.

8. Biographical sources used by Rölvaag in *Giants in the Earth* are traced in Kristoffer F. Paulson, "Berdahl Family History and Rölvaag's Immigrant History," *Norwegian-American Studies and Records* 27 (1977):55–76.

9. The manuscript for the "Viking" piece is to be found in Box 26 of the Rölvaag collection in the Norwegian-American Historical Association archives, St. Olaf College, Northfield, Minnesota (hereafter cited as NAHA); it was published in *American Magazine* (October 1929) with the title "The Vikings of the Middle West." The occasion of his last public appearance was a talk given on 2 October 1931 to the Committee (of which he was secretary) on Planning a Norwegian-American Exhibit at the Century of Progress Exhibition of 1933.

10. Alexis de Tocqueville, *Democracy in America* (New York: Alfred A. Knopf, 1945), 2:74.

11. Robert L. Heilbroner, *The Future as History* (New York: Harper and Row, 1968), p. 19.

12. Mircea Eliade, *The Myth of the Eternal Return,* trans. Willard R. Trask (Princeton, N.J.: Bollingen Series 46, 1954).

13. Frederick Jackson Turner, "The West and American Ideals," in *The Frontier in American History* (New York: Holt, Rinehart and Winston, 1962), p. 293. Regarding some of the questions raised by Turner's theory, see George W. Pierson, "The Frontier and American Institutions: A Criticism of the Turner Theory," *New England Quarterly* 15 (June 1942):224.

14. Sören Kierkegaard, *Concluding Unscientific Postscript,* trans. David F. Swenson (Princeton, NJ: Princeton University Press, 1941), p. 18.

15. Einar I. Haugen, "O. E. Rölvaag: Norwegian-American," *Norwegian-American Studies and Records* 7 (1933):53.

16. Theodore C. Blegen, *Grass Roots History* (Minneapolis: University of Minnesota Press, 1947), p. 104.

17. O. E. Rölvaag, *Giants in the Earth,* trans. Lincoln Colcord (New York: Harper and Row, 1965), pp. 32, 241, 152, 153. All subsequent references to this novel are by page number in parentheses within the text.

18. A much-needed correction to the myth critics of the American West is Christer Lennart Mosberg, "Shucking the Pastoral Ideal: Sources and Meaning of Realism in Scandinavian Immigrant Fiction about the Pioneer Farm Experience," in *Where the West Begins,* eds. Arthur R. Huseboe and William Geyer (Sioux Falls, S.D.: Center for Western Studies Press, 1978), pp. 42–50. Another perceptive study in the same direction is Charles Boewe, "Rölvaag's America: An Immigrant Novelist's Views," *Western Humanities Review* 2 (Winter 1957):3–12.

19. Sacvan Bercovitch theorizes that in American Romanticism the doctrine of *sola fide* was subsumed into *exemplum fidei.* See his *The Puritan Origins of the American Self* (New Haven, Conn.: Yale University Press, 1975), p. 164.

20. Kierkegaard, *The Concept of Dread,* trans. Walter Lowrie (Princeton, N.J.: Princeton University Press, 1957), pp. 110–15.

21. Theodore Jorgenson and Nora O. Solum, *Ole Edvart Rölvaag: A Biography* (New York: Harper and Brothers, 1939), p. 147.

22. John Heitmann, "Ole Edvart Rölvaag," *Norwegian-American Studies and Records* 12 (1941):157–58. Rölvaag's daughter, Ella Valborg Tweet, has alluded to the affection her father had for the Heitmann brothers (John and Hans) whose boyhood home in Akvik, on the eastern shore of Dönna, housed the community library where the boys "spent endless hours reading books." The most difficult ones such as *Either/Or*, she said, they "read aloud and discussed, and tried to discover their significance." "Recollections of My Father, O. E. Rölvaag," *Minnesota English Journal* 8 (Winter 1972):6.

23. Gundrun Hovde Gvåle, *O. E. Rölvaag: Nordmann og Amerikanar* (Oslo: Universitetsforlaget, 1962), pp. 85–86, 257.

24. Sören Kierkegaard, *Either/Or*, trans. Walter Lowrie (Princeton, N.J.: Princeton University Press, 1944), 2:138.

25. Jorgenson and Solum, *Ole Edvart Rölvaag*, p. 271.

26. Ibid., pp. 271, 273. The full and fascinating statement can be found in the Rölvaag Collection (Vol. 11, Box 21), NAHA.

27. Quoted in Robert Bretall, ed., *A Kierkegaard Anthology* (New York: Random House, 1959), p. 19.

28. Henrik Ibsen, *Brand*, trans. Michael Meyer (New York: Doubleday, 1960), p. 140.

29. Jonathan Edwards, *Freedom of the Will*, ed. Paul Ramsey (New Haven, Conn.: Yale University Press, 1957), pp. 137–48.

30. Kierkegaard, *Purity of Heart Is to Will One Thing*, trans. Douglas V. Steere (New York: Harper and Row, 1956), pp. 59–60.

31. Ibid., p. 121.

32. Rölvaag's title was "At Ville et er hvad." The manuscript is found in the Rölvaag Collection, NAHA. Jorgenson and Solum, who thought Rölvaag's speech original, discuss it in *Ole Edvart Rölvaag*, pp. 116–18.

33. In addition to the many things Kierkegaard wrote concerning the categories of the aesthetic, ethical, and religious, certain specific references to art and religion are found in: *Purity of Heart*, p. 27; *The Sickness Unto Death*, trans. Walter Lowrie (Princeton: Princeton University Press, 1941), pp. 123–26; *Concluding Unscientific Postscript*, pp. 347–48; *Journals and Papers*, eds. and trans. Howard V. Hong and Edna H. Hong (Bloomington: Indiana University Press, 1967), 1:63–64.

34. Seeing Ibsen as clearly attempting to render religious experience in art, Rölvaag analyzed *Peer Gynt* in terms of Kierkegaard's three categories: aesthetic, ethical, religious. Regarding the third, Rölvaag wrote: "But *religiously*, the drama glorifies the efficacy of unselfish sacrifice. We might state the ideal thus: 'Take up your cross and follow me!' " ("Christian Doctrine in Ibsen's 'Peer Gynt' [A Study of Egotism]," *Religion in Life* 1 (Winter 1932):89.

35. Jorgenson and Solum, *Ole Edvart Rölvaag*, pp. 209, 265.

36. Ibid., p. 350.

37. Ibid., p. 51.

38. Kierkegaard, *Fear and Trembling,* trans. Walter Lowrie (Princeton, N.J.: Princeton University Press, 1945), p. 47.

39. Kierkegaard, *Concluding Unscientific Postscript,* p. 386.

40. Kierkegaard, *Training in Christianity,* trans. Walter Lowrie (Princeton, N.J.: Princeton University Press, 1944), pp. 79–144.

41. Ibid., p. 100.

42. Ibid., p. 103.

43. Gvåle, p. 411.

44. Rölvaag, "Christian Doctrine . . . ," p. 89.

45. Hugh T. Kerr, ed., *A Compend of Luther's Theology* (Philadelphia: Westminster Press, 1943), p. 87.

46. Jorgenson and Solum, *Ole Edvart Rölvaag,* p. 385.

47. Ibid., p. 385.

48. Rölvaag to Lincoln Colcord (26 December 1929), Rölvaag Collection (Box 5), NAHA.

49. O. E. Rölvaag, "On Writing," manuscript, Rölvaag Collection (Box 26), NAHA, p. 22.

50. Ibid.

Chapter 4

1. Frederick Jackson Turner, "The Significance of the Frontier in American History," in *The Frontier in American History* (New York: Holt, Rinehart and Winston, 1962), p. 4.

2. Ray Allen Billington, *Frederick Jackson Turner: Historian, Scholar, Teacher* (New York: Oxford University Press, 1973), pp. 435, 454.

3. William Everson, *Archetype West: The Pacific Coast as a Literary Region* (Berkeley, Calif.: Oyez, 1976), p. 7. As a poet of many volumes Everson has also used the name Brother Antoninus.

4. The critical literature on this subject is vast, but of more than routine value are the following studies: Harvey Lewis Carter and Marcia Carpenter Spencer, "Stereotypes of the Mountain Man," *Western Historical Quarterly* 6 (January 1975):17–32; William H. Goetzmann, "The Mountain Man as Jacksonian Man," *American Quarterly* 15 (Fall 1963):402–15; Don D. Walker, "The Mountain Man as Literary Hero," *Western American Literature* 1 (Spring 1966):15–25; Max Westbrook, "The Practical Spirit: Sacrality and the American West," *Western American Literature* 3 (Fall 1968):193–205; George Woodcock, "The Lure of the Primitive," *American Scholar* 45 (Summer 1976):387–402.

5. Don Berry, *Trask* (New York: Viking Press, 1960), p. 365.

6. Everson, *Archetype West,* p. 21.

7. Ibid., p. 152.

8. Ibid., pp. 75–76.

9. Thomas J. Lyon, *John Muir,* Boise State College Western Writers Series, no. 3, (Boise, Idaho, 1972), pp. 13, 15; Roderick Nash, *Wilderness and the American Mind* (New Haven: Yale University Press, 1967), p. 123; Kevin Starr, *Americans and the California Dream, 1850–1915* (New York: Oxford University Press, 1973), p. 185.

10. William Frederic Badè, *The Life and Letters of John Muir* (Boston: Houghton Mifflin, 1923), 1:58, 63, 145; John Muir, *Letters to a Friend: Written to Mrs. Ezra S. Carr, 1866–1879* (Boston: Houghton Mifflin, 1915), pp. 1, 2.

11. John Muir, *The Story of My Boyhood and Youth* (Madison: University of Wisconsin Press, 1965), pp. 27, 63; Badè, 1:19.

12. John Muir, *A Thousand-Mile Walk to the Gulf* (Boston: Houghton Mifflin, 1916), pp. 16, 30, 212.

13. Herbert F. Smith, *John Muir* (New York: Twayne, 1965), p. 54.

14. John Muir, *My First Summer in the Sierra* (Boston: Houghton Mifflin, 1916), pp. 73, 146, 39, 250; Badè, *Life and Letters*, 1:218, 213.

15. Badè, *Life and Letters*, 1:2:31.

16. Ibid., 1:271, 21; Linnie Marsh Wolfe, ed., *John of the Mountains: The Unpublished Journals of John Muir* (Boston: Houghton Mifflin, 1938), p. xvii; Badè, *Life and Letters*, 1:325; Wolfe, p. xvii. For Muir's several letters to Emerson see Ralph L. Rusk, ed., *The Letters of Ralph Waldo Emerson* (New York: Columbia University Press, 1939), 4:154–57, 202–4.

17. Badè, *Life and Letters*, 2:28–29.

18. Wolfe, *John of the Mountains*, p. 95; Badè, *Life and Letters*, 2:7, 6, 117–18.

19. Badè, *Life and Letters*, 2:306, 317–18, 342–43; Wolfe, *John of the Mountains*, p. xvi.

20. Quoted references are to M. H. Abrams, *Natural Supernaturalism: Tradition and Revolution in Romantic Literature* (New York: W. W. Norton, 1971), pp. 69, 65.

21. Wolfe, *John of the Mountains*, p. 304.

22. John Muir, *Travels in Alaska* (Boston: Houghton Mifflin, 1915), p. 198.

23. Samuel Hall Young, *Alaska Days with John Muir* (New York: Fleming H. Revell, 1915), pp. 63–64, 110, 117–18; Muir, *Travels in Alaska*, pp. 152, 153; cf. Henry David Thoreau, *Walden*, "The Ponds" and "Spring."

24. John Muir, *The Cruise of the Corwin* (Boston: Houghton Mifflin, 1917), p. 109.

25. Wolfe, *John of the Mountains*, p. 191; Muir, *Letters to a Friend*, p. 81.

26. Badè, *Life and Letters*, 2:210, 211; Wolfe, *John of the Mountains*, pp. 337–38.

27. Lyon, *John Muir*, p. 16; Wolfe, *John of the Mountains*, pp. 77, 89.

28. Badè, *Life and Letters*, 2:279.

29. Ibid., 354.

30. Ibid., 364; Wolfe, *John of the Mountains*, p. 439.

Chapter 5

1. Sydney E. Ahlstrom, ed., *Theology in America: The Major Protestant Voices from Puritanism to Neo-Orthodoxy* (Indianapolis, Ind.: Bobbs-Merrill, 1967), p. 463.

2. Josiah Royce, *The Sources of Religious Insight* (New York: Charles Scribner's Sons, 1912), pp. 261–62, 270–71, 272–73.

Notes

3. For additional exposition about these two terms, see M. H. Abrams, *Natural Supernaturalism: Tradition and Revolution in Romantic Literature* (New York: W. W. Norton, 1971), chap. 3.

4. Paul Fussell, *The Great War and Modern Memory* (New York: Oxford University Press, 1975), chap. 2.

5. Unless otherwise noted, references to Frost's poems are to *Complete Poems of Robert Frost* (New York: Holt, Rinehart and Winston, 1964).

6. Norman H. Holland, "Psychological Depths and 'Dover Beach,'" *Victorian Studies* 9 (September 1965):5–28.

7. Lionel Trilling, "A Speech on Robert Frost: A Cultural Episode," *Partisan Review* 26 (Summer 1959):445–52.

8. Trilling, *Beyond Culture: Essays on Literature and Learning* (New York: Viking Press, 1968), pp. 3–30.

9. Ibid., p. 27.

10. Lawrance Thompson and R. H. Winnick, *Robert Frost: The Later Years, 1938–1963* (New York: Holt, Rinehart and Winston, 1976), p. 22. Subsequent citations to Thompson's three-volume biography (volume 3 completed by Winnick) appear within the text.

11. "Remarks Accepting the Gold Medal of the National Institute of Arts & Letters," in *Selected Prose of Robert Frost*, eds. Hyde Cox and Edward Connery Lathen (New York: Collier Books, 1968), p. 102.

12. "The Imp of the Perverse," in *Selected Writings of Edgar Allan Poe*, ed. Edward H. Davidson (Boston: Houghton Mifflin, 1956), p. 228.

13. Louise Bogan, *Achievement in American Poetry: 1900–1950* (Chicago: Henry Regnery, 1951), pp. 47–51; Yvor Winters, "Robert Frost: Or, the Spiritual Drifter as Poet," *Sewanee Review* 56 (August 1948):564–96; Roy Harvey Pearce, *The Continuity of American Poetry* (Princeton, N.J.: Princeton University Press, 1961), p. 282; Randall Jarrell, *Poetry and the Age* (New York: Alfred A. Knopf, 1953), p. 31; Frederic I. Carpenter, review of Frost's *Collected Poems*, in *New England Quarterly* 5 (January 1932):159–60. The views of these so-called negative critics are assessed in Donald J. Greiner, *Robert Frost: The Poet and His Critics* (Chicago: American Library Association, 1974), chap. 3.

14. George W. Nitchie, *Human Values in the Poetry of Robert Frost: A Study of a Poet's Convictions* (Durham, N.C.: Duke University Press, 1960), pp. 185–86, 218.

15. "The Figure a Poem Makes," *Selected Prose* pp. 18, 20.

16. For discussion of these interpolations, see Marion Montgomery, "Robert Frost and His Use of Barriers: Man vs. Nature Toward God," *The South Atlantic Quarterly* 57 (Summer 1958):339–53.

17. "The Figure a Poem Makes," p. 20.

18. James M. Cox, "Robert Frost and the Edge of the Clearning," *Virginia Quarterly Review* 35 (Winter 1959):87.

19. Hayden Carruth, "The New England Tradition," *American Libraries* 2 (October 1971):945.

20. André Gide, *Dostoevsky* (London: Secker & Warburg, 1952), p. 143.

Chapter 6

1. Quotations are taken from Reinhold Niebuhr, *The Nature and Destiny of Man: A Christian Interpretation* (New York: Charles Scribner's Sons, 1941), pp. 186–87, and ideas touched on in this paragraph are developed at length in his chaps. 1–7.

2. Reinhold Niebuhr, *Moral Man and Immoral Society* (New York: Charles Scribner's Sons, 1932), p. 69.

3. Erich Kahler, *The Orbit of Thomas Mann* (Princeton, N.J.: Princeton University Press, 1969), p. 113.

4. Ibid., p. 116.

5. John Calvin, *Institutes of the Christian Religion*, trans. Ford Lewis Battles and ed. John T. McNeill (Philadelphia: Westminster Press, 1960), 2:274–75. A lucid explication of Calvin's defense of secular learning (*Institutes*, 2:271–76) is found in the epilogue ("An Essay on Calvin's Defense of Secular Studies: His Doctrine of Common Grace") of Quirinus Breen's *John Calvin: A Study in French Humanism*, 2d ed. (Hamden, Conn.: Archon Books, 1968), pp. 165–79.

6. M. P. Ramsey, *Calvin and Art* (Edinburgh: Moray Press, 1938), p. 15.

7. T. E. Hulme, "Humanism and the Religious Attitude," in *Speculations* (London: Routledge and Kegan Paul, 1960), chap. 1.

8. Richard Kroner, *Speculation and Revelation in the Age of Christian Philosophy* (Philadelphia: Westminister Press, 1959), pp. 190–95. The same idea finds its modern expression in Barthian theology. "Faith," says Barth, "can never be lived except in a Notwithstanding: notwithstanding all that man finds himself and his fellow-men to be, notwithstanding all that he and his fellow-men may try to do" (*Church Dogmatics*, vol. 4, pt. 1, eds. G. W. Bromiley and T. F. Torrance [Edinburgh: T. and T. Clarke, 1956], p. 635).

9. The bibliography on this subject is extensive. Still the best recent survey of relevant studies is found in Amos Wilder's introduction to his *Early Christian Rhetoric: The Language of the Gospel* (Cambridge, Mass.: Harvard University Press, 1971). His earlier volume, *Theology and Modern Literature* (Cambridge, Mass.: Harvard University Press, 1958), is useful. The most prolific scholar in the field is Nathan A. Scott, Jr. Other noteworthy studies are: Sallie TeSelle, *Literature and the Christian Life* (New Haven, Conn.: Yale University Press, 1966); T. R. Henn, *The Bible as Literature* (London: Oxford University Press, 1970); G. B. Tennyson and Edward E. Ericson, Jr., eds. *Religion and Modern Literature* (Grand Rapids, Mich.: William B. Eerdmans, 1975).

10. Austin Farrer argues that analysis of the Gospel of St. Mark "belongs plainly to the criticism of poetry," which is its genre (*The Glass of Vision* [London: Dacre Press, 1948], p. 145). Although Helen Gardner attacks Farrer on several points, she also thinks that "reading the Gospel is like reading a poem" (*The Business of Criticism* [London: Oxford University Press, 1959], p. 102). For an analysis of the Bible as archetype, see Northrop Frye, *The Anatomy of Criticism: Four Essays* (Princeton, N.J.: Princeton University Press, 1957), pp. 315–26.

11. John W. Dixon, "The Matter of Theology: The Consequences of Art for Theological Method," *Journal of Religion* 49 (April 1969):173.

12. Paul Tillich, *Theology of Culture,* ed. Robert C. Kimball (New York: Oxford University Press, 1959), p. 68. See Gabriel Vahanian, "Picasso's Iconoclasm," *Christian Century* 88 (29 December 1971):1523–25.

13. T. S. Eliot, *The Sacred Wood: Essays on Poetry and Criticism* (London: Methuen, 1920), pp. 144–55.

14. Samuel Perkins Hayes, "An Historical Study of the Edwardean Revivals," *The American Journal of Psychology* 13 (October 1902):558; Joseph Haroutunian, "Jonathan Edwards: Theologian of the Great Commandment," *Theology Today* 1 (April 1944):367; Edwin H. Cady, "The Artistry of Jonathan Edwards," *New England Quarterly* 22 (March 1949):61–72; Roland Delattre, *Beauty and Sensibility in the Thought of Jonathan Edwards: An Essay in Aesthetics and Theological Ethics* (New Haven: Yale University Press, 1968).

15. E. M. W. Tillyard and C. S. Lewis, *The Personal Heresy: A Controversy* (London: Oxford University Press, 1965), p. 89.

16. Haroutunian, "Jonathan Edwards: Theologian of the Great Commandment," p. 368.

17. This point is discussed in Gerardus van der Leeuw, *Sacred and Profane Beauty: The Holy in Art,* trans. David E. Green (New York: Holt, Rinehart and Winston, 1963), p. 284. See also Paul Tillich, "Existentialist Aspects of Modern Art," in *Christianity and the Existentialists,* ed. Carl Michalson (New York: Charles Scribner's Sons, 1956), pp. 128–47.

18. Jonathan Edwards, "Unbelievers Contemn the Glory and Excellency of Christ," *Works,* ed. Edward Hickman (London: F. Westley and A. H. Davis, 1834), 2:61.

19. W. H. Auden, *The Dyer's Hand and Other Essays* (New York: Random House, 1962), p. 457.

20. C. S. Lewis, *Christian Reflections,* ed. Walter Hooper (Grand Rapids, Mich.: William B. Eerdmans, 1967), p. 67.

21. George Santayana, *Interpretation of Poetry and Religion* (New York: Harper and Brothers, 1957), pp. 92, 94.

22. Jonathan Edwards, *A Treatise Concerning Religious Affections,* ed. John E. Smith (New Haven, Conn.: Yale University Press, 1959), p. 275.

23. Santayana, p. 89; G. Wilson Knight, *The Christian Renaissance* (New York: W. W. Norton, 1962), p. 32; Kroner, *Speculation and Revelation,* p. 47.

24. C. S. Lewis, *Rehabilitation and Other Essays* (London: Oxford University Press, 1939), p. 195.

25. M. H. Abrams, *The Mirror and the Lamp: Romantic Theory and the Critical Tradition* (New York: Oxford University Press, 1953).

26. C. S. Lewis, *Rehabilitation,* pp. 191–92.

27. Howard Mumford Jones, *The Bright Medusa* (Urbana: University of Illinois Press, 1952), pp. 39–40.

28. William Faulkner, *The Sound and the Fury* and *As I Lay Dying* (New York: Random House, 1946), p. 196.

29. Paul Fussell, *The Great War and Modern Memory* (New York: Oxford University Press, 1975), p. 209.

30. Ibid., p. 29.

31. Ibid.

32. Quoted in Fussell, *The Great War and Modern Memory*, p. 63.

33. Norman Foerster, "The Esthetic Judgment and Ethical Judgment," in *The Intent of the Critic*, ed. Donald A. Stauffer (Princeton, N.J.: Princeton University Press, 1941), p. 88.

34. Douglas Bush, "The Humanist Critic," *Kenyon Review* 13 (1951):86.

35. Douglas Bush, *Prefaces to Renaissance Literature* (New York: W. W. Norton, 1965), pp. 93–94.

36. R. W. B. Lewis, *The Picaresque Saint: Representative Figures in Contemporary Literature* (Philadelphia: Lippincott, 1961), p. 17.

37. Wylie Sypher, *Loss of the Self in Modern Literature and Art* (New York: Random House, 1962), p. 154.

38. W. K. Wimsatt, Jr. and Monroe C. Beardsley, "The Intentional Fallacy," in Wimsatt, *The Verbal Icon: Studies in the Meaning of Poetry* (Lexington: University of Kentucky Press, 1967), p. 4.

39. See Sarah Lawall, *Critics of Consciousness: The Existential Structure of Literature* (Cambridge, Mass.: Harvard University Press, 1968).

40. Paul de Man, *Blindness & Insight: Essays in the Rhetoric of Contemporary Criticism* (New York: Oxford University Press, 1971), p. 49.

41. Lionel Trilling, *Sincerity and Authenticity* (Cambridge, Mass.: Harvard University Press, 1972), p. 99.

42. Ibid.

43. Geoffrey H. Hartman, *Beyond Formalism: Literary Essays. 1958–1970* (New Haven, Conn.: Yale University Press, 1970), p. 53.

44. Murray Krieger, *The Tragic Vision: Variations on a Theme in Literary Interpretation* (Chicago: University of Chicago Press, 1966), chaps. 8.

45. James Guetti, *The Limits of Metaphor: A Study of Melville, Conrad, and Faulkner* (Ithaca, N.Y.: Cornell University Press, 1960), pp. 173, 178–79.

46. See Walter J. Slatoff, *Quest for Failure: A Study of William Faulkner* (Ithaca, N.Y.: Cornell University Press, 1960).

47. C. G. Jung, *Psychology of the Unconscious* (New York: Dodd, Mead, 1965), p. 199.

48. William Barrett, *Time of Need: Forms of Imagination in the Twentieth Century* (New York: Harper and Row, 1972), p. 232.

49. Maud Bodkin, *Archetypal Patterns in Poetry: Psychological Studies of Imagination* (London: Oxford University Press, 1934), p. 278.

50. See Georg Lukács, *Realism in Our Time: Literature and the Class Struggle*, trans. John and Necke Mander (New York: Harper and Row, 1971). Lukács admonishes to be done with an angst-ridden vision, to cast off allegory and subjectivity, and to live in objective history with "actual persons inhabiting a palpable, identifiable world" (p. 24).

51. Mircea Eliade, *No Souvenirs: Journal 1957–1969*, trans. Fred H. Johnson (New York: Harper and Row, 1977), p. 71.

52. Ibid., pp. 164–65.

53. See Reinhold Niebuhr, *The Irony of American History* (New York: Charles Scribner's Sons, 1952), p. 63.

Bibliography

Abrams, M. H. *The Mirror and the Lamp: Romantic Theory and the Critical Tradition.* New York: Oxford University Press, 1953.

———. *Natural Supernaturalism: Tradition and Revolution in Romantic Literature.* New York: W. W. Norton, 1971.

Ahlstrom, Sydney E., ed. *Theology in America: The Major Protestant Voices from Puritanism to Neo-Orthodoxy.* Indianapolis, Ind.: Bobbs-Merrill, 1967.

Auden, W. H. *The Dyer's Hand and Other Essays.* New York: Random House, 1962.

Badè, William Frederic. *The Life and Letters of John Muir.* 2 vols. Boston: Houghton Mifflin, 1923.

Barrett, William. *Time of Need: Forms of the Imagination in the Twentieth Century.* New York: Harper and Row, 1972.

Barth, Karl. *Church Dogmatics.* Edited by G. W. Bromiley and T. F. Torrance. Vol. 4. Edinburgh: T. and T. Clark, 1956.

Bell, Millicent. *Hawthorne's View of the Artist.* Albany: State University of New York Press, 1962.

Bercovitch, Sacvan. *The Puritan Origins of the American Self.* New Haven, Conn.: Yale University Press, 1975.

———, ed. *The American Puritan Imagination: Essays in Revaluation.* London: Cambridge University Press, 1974.

Berry, Don. *Trask.* New York: Viking Press, 1960.

Billington, Ray Allen. *Frederick Jackson Turner: Historian, Scholar, Teacher.* New York: Oxford University Press, 1973.

Blegen, Theodore C. *Grass Roots History.* Minneapolis: University of Minnesota Press, 1947.

Bodkin, Maud. *Archetypal Patterns in Poetry: Psychological Studies of Imagination*. London: Oxford University Press, 1934.

Boewe, Charles. "Rölvaag's America: An Immigrant Novelist's Views." *Western Humanities Review* 2 (Winter 1957): 3–12.

Bogan, Louise. *Achievement in American Poetry: 1900–1950*. Chicago: Henry Regnery, 1951.

Bojer, Johan. *The Great Hunger*. Translated by W. J. Alexander Worster and C. Archer. New York: Grosset, 1919.

Bradford, William. *Of Plymouth Plantation, 1620–1647*. Edited by Samuel Eliot Morison. New York: Alfred A. Knopf, 1953.

Breen, Quirinus. *John Calvin: A Study in French Humanism*. 2d ed. Hamden, Conn.: Archon Books, 1968.

Bretall, Robert, ed. *A Kierkegaard Anthology*. New York: Random House, 1959.

Brumm, Ursula. *American Thought and Religious Typology*. Translated by John Hoaglund. New Brunswick, N.J.: Rutgers University Press, 1970.

Bush, Douglas. "The Humanist Critic." *Kenyon Review* 13 (1951):81–92.

———. *Prefaces to Renaissance Literature*. New York: W. W. Norton, 1965.

Cady, Edwin H. "The Artistry of Jonathan Edwards." *New England Quarterly* 22 (March 1949):61–72.

Calvin, John. *Institutes of the Christian Religion*. Edited by John T. McNeill. Translated by Ford Lewis Battles. 2 vols. Philadelphia: Westminister Press, 1960.

Carpenter, Frederic I. Review of *Collected Poems*, by Robert Frost. *New England Quarterly* 5 (January 1932): 159–60.

Carruth, Hayden. "The New England Tradition." *American Libraries* 2 (October 1971):690–700, 938–48.

Carter, Harvey Lewis, and Spencer, Marcia Carpenter. "Stereotypes of the Mountain Man." *Western Historical Quarterly* 6 (January 1975):17–32.

Cotton, John. "God's Promise to His Plantation." In *Colonial American Literature*, edited by Roy Harvey Pearce. 2d ed. New York: Holt, Rinehart and Winston, 1969.

Cox, James M. "Robert Frost and the Edge of the Clearing." *Virginia Quarterly Review* 35 (Winter 1959):73–88.

―――. "The Scarlet Letter: Through the Old Manse and the Custom House." *Virginia Quarterly Review,* 51 (Summer 1975): 432–47.

Delattre, Roland. *Beauty and Sensibility in the Thought of Jonathan Edwards: An Essay in Aesthetics and Theological Ethics.* New Haven, Conn.: Yale University Press, 1968.

Dixon, John W. "The Matter of Theology: The Consequences of Art for Theological Method." *Journal of Religion* 49 (April 1969):160–79.

Edwards, Jonathan, *Freedom of the Will.* Edited by Paul Ramsey. New Haven, Conn.: Yale University Press, 1957.

―――. *The Great Awakening.* Edited by C. C. Goen. New Haven, Conn.: Yale University Press, 1972.

―――. *Images or Shadows of Divine Things.* Edited with an introduction by Perry Miller. New Haven, Conn.: Yale University Press, 1948.

―――. "Miscellanies." In *The Philosophy of Jonathan Edwards from His Private Notebooks,* edited by Harvey G. Townsend. Eugene: University of Oregon Press, 1955.

―――. *The Nature of True Virtue.* Edited by William K. Frankena. Ann Arbor: University of Michigan Press, 1960.

―――. *Original Sin.* Edited by Clyde A. Holbrook. New Haven, Conn.: Yale University Press, 1970.

―――. *Treatise Concerning Religious Affections.* Edited by John E. Smith. New Haven, Conn.: Yale University Press, 1959.

―――. *Treatise on Grace and Other Posthumously Published Writings.* Edited by Paul Helm. Cambridge and London: James Clarke, 1971.

―――. *Works.* Edited by Edward Hickman. 2 vols. London: F. Westley and A. H. Davis, 1834.

Elder, Marjorie J. *Nathaniel Hawthorne: Transcendental Symbolist.* Athens: Ohio University Press, 1969.

Eliade, Mircea. *The Myth of the Eternal Return.* Translated by Willard R. Trask. New York: Pantheon Books, 1954.

————. *No Souvenirs: Journal 1957–1969*. Translated by Fred H. Johnson. New York: Harper & Row, 1977.

Eliot, T. S. *The Sacred Wood: Essays on Poetry and Criticism*. London: Methuen, 1920.

Erikson, Erik H. *Young Man Luther: A Study in Psychoanalysis and History*. New York: W. W. Norton, 1962.

Everson, William. *Archetype West: The Pacific Coast as a Literary Region*. Berkeley, Calif.: Oyez, 1976.

Farrer, Austin. *The Glass of Vision*. London: Dacre Press, 1948.

Faulkner, William. *The Sound and the Fury* and *As I Lay Dying*. New York: Random House, 1946.

Faust, Clarence H., and Johnson, Thomas H., eds. *Jonathan Edwards: Representative Selections*. Rev. ed. New York: Hill and Wang, 1962.

Feidelson, Charles, Jr. *Symbolism and American Literature*. Chicago: University of Chicago Press, 1953.

Fichte, Johann. *Addresses to the German Nation*. Translated by R. F. Jones and G. H. Turnbull. Chicago and London: Open Court Publishing Co., 1922.

Foerster, Norman. "The Esthetic Judgment and Ethical Judgment." In *The Intent of the Critic*, edited by Donald A. Stauffer. Princeton, N.J.: Princeton University Press, 1941.

Fogle, Richard Harter. *Hawthorne's Fiction: The Light and the Dark*. Norman: University of Oklahoma Press, 1964.

Frost, Robert. *Complete Poems of Robert Frost*. New York: Holt, Rinehart and Winston, 1964.

————. *Selected Prose of Robert Frost*. Edited by Hyde Cox and Edward Connery Lathen. New York: Collier Books, 1968.

Frye, Northrop. *The Anatomy of Criticism: Four Essays*. Princeton, N.J.: Princeton University Press, 1957.

Fussell, Paul. *The Great War and Modern Memory*. New York: Oxford University Press, 1975.

Gardner, Helen. *The Business of Criticism*. London: Oxford University Press, 1959.

Gide, André. *Dostoevsky*. London: Secker and Warburg, 1952.

Goetzmann, William H. "The Mountain Man as Jacksonian Man." *American Quarterly* 15 (Fall 1963): 402–15.

Greiner, Donald J. *Robert Frost: The Poet and His Critics.* Chicago: American Library Association, 1974.

Griffith, John. "Jonathan Edwards as a Literary Artist." *Criticism* 15 (Spring 1973):156–73.

Guetti, James. *The Limits of Metaphor: A Study of Melville, Conrad, and Faulkner.* Ithaca, N.Y.: Cornell University Press, 1960.

Gvåle, Gundrun Hovde. *O. E. Rölvaag: Nordmann og Amerikanar.* Oslo: Universitetsforlaget, 1962.

Haroutunian, Joseph. "Jonathan Edwards: Theologian of the Great Commandment." *Theology Today* 1 (April 1944): 361–77.

———. *Piety Versus Moralism: The Passing of New England Theology.* New York: Harper and Row, 1970.

Hartman, Geoffrey H. *Beyond Formalism: Literary Essays, 1958–1970.* New Haven, Conn.: Yale University Press, 1970.

Haugen, Einar I. "O. E. Rölvaag: Norwegian-American." *Norwegian-American Studies and Records* 7 (1933):53–73.

Hawthorne, Nathaniel. *The Complete Works.* 12 vols. Boston: Houghton Mifflin, 1890.

———. *The Scarlet Letter.* Introduction by Austin Warren. New York: Rinehart, 1947.

Hayes, Samuel Perkins. "An Historical Study of the Edwardean Revivals." *The American Journal of Psychology* 13 (1902): 550–74.

Heilbroner, Robert L. *The Future as History.* New York: Harper and Row, 1968.

Heitmann, John. "Ole Edvart Rölvaag." *Norwegian-American Studies and Records* 12 (1941):144–66.

Henn, T. R. *The Bible as Literature.* London: Oxford University Press, 1970.

Holland, Norman H. "Psychological Depths and 'Dover Beach.'" *Victorian Studies* 9 (September 1965):5–28.

Hooker, Thomas. "A True Sight of Sin." In *The Puritans,* edited by Perry Miller and Thomas H. Johnson. Vol. 1. New York: Harper and Row, 1963.

Howard, Leon. *"The Mind" of Jonathan Edwards: A Reconstructed Text.* Berkeley: University of California Press, 1963.

Hulme, T. E. *Speculations.* London: Routledge and Kegan Paul, 1960.

Ibsen, Henrick. *Brand.* Translated by Michael Meyer. New York: Doubleday, 1960.

Jarrell, Randall. *Poetry and the Age.* New York: Alfred A. Knopf, 1953.

Jones, Howard Mumford. *The Bright Medusa.* Urbana: University of Illinois Press, 1952.

Jorgenson, Theodore, and Solum, Nora O. *Ole Edvart Rölvaag: A Biography.* New York: Harper and Brothers, 1939.

Jung, C. G. *Psychology of the Unconscious.* New York: Dodd, Mead, 1965.

Kahler, Erich. *The Orbit of Thomas Mann.* Princeton, N.J.: Princeton University Press, 1969.

Kerr, Hugh T., ed. *A Compend of Luther's Theology.* Philadelphia: Westminster Press, 1943.

Kierkegaard, Sören. *The Concept of Dread.* Translated by Walter Lowrie. Princeton, N.J.: Princeton University Press, 1957.

―――. *Concluding Unscientific Postscript.* Translated by David F. Swenson. Princeton, N.J.: Princeton University Press, 1941.

―――. *Either/Or.* 2 vols. Translated by Walter Lowrie. Princeton, N.J.: Princeton University Press, 1944.

―――. *Fear and Trembling.* Translated by Walter Lowrie. Princeton, N.J.: Princeton University Press, 1945.

―――. *Journals and Papers.* 3 vols. Edited and translated by Howard V. Hong and Edna H. Hong. Bloomington: Indiana University Press, 1967.

―――. *Purity of Heart Is to Will One Thing.* Translated by Douglas V. Steere. New York: Harper and Row, 1956.

―――. *The Sickness Unto Death.* Translated by Walter Lowrie. Princeton, N.J.: Princeton University Press, 1941.

―――. *Training in Christianity.* Translated by Walter Lowrie. Princeton, N.J.: Princeton University Press, 1944.

Knight, G. Wilson. *The Christian Renaissance.* New York: W. W. Norton, 1962.

Kolodny, Annette. "Imagery in the Sermons of Jonathan Edwards." *Early American Literature* 13 (Fall 1972):172–82.

Krieger, Murray. *The Tragic Vision: Variations on a Theme in Literary Interpretation.* Chicago: University of Chicago Press, 1966.

Kroner, Richard. *Speculation and Revelation in the Age of Christian Philosophy.* Philadelphia: Westminster Press, 1959.

————. *The Religious Function of Imagination.* New Haven, Conn.: Yale University Press, 1941.

Lawall, Sarah. *Critics of Consciousness: The Existential Structure of Literature.* Cambridge, Mass.: Harvard University Press, 1968.

Leeuw, Gerardus van der. *Sacred and Profane Beauty: The Holy in Art.* Translated by David E. Green. New York: Holt, Rinehart and Winston, 1963.

Lewis, C. S. *Christian Reflections.* Edited by Walter Hooper. Grand Rapids, Mich.: William B. Eerdmans, 1967.

————. *Rehabilitation and Other Essays.* London: Oxford University Press, 1939.

Lewis, R. W. B. *The American Adam: Innocence, Tragedy, and Tradition in the Nineteenth Century.* Chicago: University of Chicago Press, 1955.

————. *The Picaresque Saint: Representative Figures in Contemporary Literature.* Philadelphia: Lippincott, 1961.

Leyda, Jay. *The Melville Log.* 2 vols. New York: Gordian Press, 1969.

Locke, John. *An Essay Concerning Human Understanding.* London: G. Offor et al, 1819.

Lowance, Mason I., Jr. " 'Images or Shadows of Divine Things' in the Thought of Jonathan Edwards." In *Typology and Early American Literature,* edited by Sacvan Bercovitch. Amherst: University of Massachusetts Press, 1972.

Lukács, Georg. *Realism in Our Time: Literature and the Class Struggle.* Translated by John and Necke Mander. New York: Harper and Row, 1971.

Lyon, Thomas J. *John Muir.* Boise State College Western Writers Series, no. 3, Boise, Idaho, 1972.

Man, Paul de. *Blindness & Insight: Essays in the Rhetoric of Contemporary Criticism.* New York: Oxford University Press, 1971.

Mather, Samuel. *Figures or Types of the Old Testament.* 1683. Reprint. New York: Johnson Reprint, 1969.

Matthiessen, F. O. *American Renaissance: Art and Expression in the Age of Emerson and Whitman.* New York: Oxford University Press, 1941.

Melville, Herman. "Hawthorne and His Mosses." In *The Art of the Essay,* edited by Leslie Fiedler. New York: Thomas Y. Crowell, 1958.

Miller, Perry. *Errand Into the Wilderness.* New York: Harper and Row, 1964.

———. "Jonathan Edwards on the Sense of the Heart." *Harvard Theological Review* 41 (1948):123–45.

———. *The New England Mind: The Seventeenth Century.* Cambridge, Mass.: Harvard University Press, 1963.

Montgomery, Marion. "Robert Frost and His Use of Barriers: Man vs. Nature Toward God." *The South Atlantic Quarterly* 57 (Summer 1958):339–53.

Mossberg, Christer Lennart. "Shucking the Pastoral Ideal: Sources and Meaning of Realism in Scandinavian Immigrant Fiction about the Pioneer Farm Experience." In *Where the West Begins,* edited by Authur R. Huseboe and William Geyer. Sioux Falls, S.D.: Center for Western Studies Press, 1978.

Muir, John. *The Cruise of the Corwin.* Boston: Houghton Mifflin, 1917.

———. *Letters to a Friend: Written to Mrs. Ezra S. Carr, 1866–1879.* Boston: Houghton Mifflin, 1915.

———. *My First Summer in the Sierra.* Boston: Houghton Mifflin, 1916.

———. *The Story of My Boyhood and Youth.* Madison: University of Wisconsin, 1965.

———. *A Thousand-Mile Walk to the Gulf.* Boston: Houghton Mifflin, 1915.

———. *Travels in Alaska.* Boston: Houghton Mifflin, 1915.

Nash, Roderick. *Wilderness and the American Mind.* New Haven, Conn.: Yale University Press, 1967.

Niebuhr, H. Richard. *The Meaning of Revelation.* New York: Macmillan, 1941.

Niebuhr, Reinhold. *The Irony of American History.* New York: Charles Scribner's Sons, 1952.

———. *Moral Man and Immoral Society.* New York: Charles Scribner's Sons, 1932.

———. *The Nature and Destiny of Man: A Christian Interpretation.* New York: Charles Scribner's Sons, 1941.

Nitchie, George W. *Human Values in the Poetry of Robert Frost: A Study of a Poet's Convictions.* Durham, N.C.: Duke University Press, 1960.

Otto, Rudolf. *The Idea of the Holy.* 2d ed. Translated by John W. Harvey. London: Oxford University Press, 1950.

Parrington, Vernon Louis. *Main Currents in American Thought.* Vol. 1. New York: Harcourt Brace, 1926.

Pauck, William. *The Heritage of the Reformation.* Boston: Beacon Press, 1950.

Paulson, Kristoffer F. "Berdahl Family History and Rölvaag's Immigrant History." *Norwegian-American Studies and Records* 27 (1977):55–76.

Pearce, Roy Harvey. *The Continuity of American Poetry.* Princeton, N.J.: Princeton University Press, 1961.

Pierson, George W. "The Frontier and American Institutions: A Criticism of the Turner Theory." *New England Quarterly* 15 (June 1942):224–55.

Poe, Edgar Allan. *Selected Writings of Edgar Allan Poe.* Edited by Edward H. Davidson. Boston: Houghton Mifflin, 1956.

Ramsey, M. P. *Calvin and Art.* Edinburgh: Moray Press, 1938.

Rölvaag, O. E. *The Boat of Longing.* Translated by Nora Solum. New York: Harper and Brothers, 1933.

———. "Christian Doctrine in Ibsen's 'Peer Gynt' (A Study of Egotism)." *Religion in Life* 1 (Winter 1932):70–89.

———. *Giants in the Earth.* Translated by Lincoln Colcord. New York: Harper and Row, 1965.

———. *The Third Life of Per Smevik.* Translated by Ella Valborg Tweet and Solveig Zempel. Minneapolis, Minn.: Dillon Press, 1971.

Royce, Josiah. *The Sources of Religious Insight.* New York: Charles Scribner's Sons, 1912.

Rusk, Ralph, ed. *The Letters of Ralph Waldo Emerson.* New York: Columbia University Press, 1939. Vol. VI.

Santayana, George. *Interpretation of Poetry and Religion.* New York: Harper and Brothers, 1957.

Slatoff, Walter J. *Quest for Failure: A Study of William Faulkner.* Ithaca, N.Y.: Cornell University Press, 1960.

Smith, Herbert F. *John Muir.* New York: Twayne, 1965.

Starr, Kevin. *Americans and the California Dream, 1850–1915.* New York: Oxford University Press, 1973.

Sypher, Wylie. *Loss of the Self in Modern Literature and Art.* New York: Random House, 1962.

Tennyson, G. B., and Ericson, Edward E., Jr., eds. *Religion and Modern Literature.* Grand Rapids, Mich.: William B. Eerdmans, 1975.

TeSelle, Sallie. *Literature and the Christian Life.* New Haven, Conn.: Yale University Press, 1966.

Thompson, Lawrance. *Robert Frost: The Early Years, 1874–1915.* New York: Holt, Rinehart and Winston, 1966.

———. *Robert Frost: The Years of Triumph, 1915–1938.* New York: Holt, Rinehart and Winston, 1970.

———, and Winnick, R. H. *Robert Frost: The Later Years, 1938–1963.* New York: Holt, Rinehart and Winston, 1976.

Tillich, Paul. "Existentialist Aspects of Modern Art." In *Christianity and the Existentialists,* edited by Carl Michalson. New York: Charles Scribner's Sons, 1956.

———. *The Protestant Era.* Abridged ed. Translated by James Luther Adams. Chicago: University of Chicago Press, 1957.

———. *Theology of Culture.* Edited by Robert C. Kimball. New York: Oxford University Press, 1959.

Tocqueville, Alexis de. *Democracy in America.* 2 vols. New York: Alfred A. Knopf, 1945.

Trilling, Lionel. *Beyond Culture: Essays on Literature and Learning.* New York: Viking Press, 1968.

———. *Sincerity and Authenticity.* Cambridge, Mass.: Harvard University Press, 1972.

———. "A Speech on Robert Frost: A Cultural Episode." *Partisan Review* 26 (Summer 1959):445–52.

Turner, Frederick Jackson. "The Significance of the Frontier in American History." In *The Frontier in American History.* New York: Holt, Rinehart and Winston, 1962.

———. "The West and American Ideals." In *The Frontier in American History.* New York: Holt, Rinehart and Winston, 1962.

Tuveson, Ernest Lee. *The Imagination as a Means of Grace: Locke and the Aesthetics of Romanticism.* Berkeley: University of California Press, 1960.

Tweet, Ella Valborg. "Recollections of My Father, O. E. Rölvaag." *Minnesota English Journal* 8 (Winter 1972):4–16.

Vahanian, Gabriel. "Picasso's Iconoclasm." *Christian Century* 88 (29 December 1971):1523–25.

Van Doren, Mark. *Nathaniel Hawthorne.* New York: William Sloane Associates, 1949.

Waggoner, Hyatt H. "Art and Belief." In *Hawthorne Centenary Essays,* edited by Roy Harvey Pearce. Columbus: Ohio State University Press, 1964.

Walker, Don D. "The Mountain Man as Literary Hero." *Western American Literature* 1 (Spring 1966):15–25.

Westbrook, Max. "The Practical Spirit: Sacrality and the American West." *Western American Literature* 3 (Fall 1968):193–205.

Wilder, Amos. *Early Christian Rhetoric: The Language of the Gospel.* Cambridge, Mass.: Harvard University Press, 1971.

———. *Theology and Modern Literature.* Cambridge, Mass.: Harvard University Press, 1958.

Wimsatt, W. K., Jr., and Beardsley, Monroe. "The Intentional Fallacy." In *The Verbal Icon: Studies in the Meaning of Poetry.* Lexington: University of Kentucky Press, 1967.

Winters, Yvor. "Robert Frost: Or, the Spiritual Drifter as Poet." *Sewanee Review* 56 (August 1948):564–96.

———. *In Defense of Reason.* Denver, Colo.: Alan Swallow, n.d.

Winthrop, John. "A Model of Christian Charity." In *Colonial American Writing,* edited by Roy Harvey Pearce. 2d ed. New York: Holt, Rinehart and Winston, 1969.

Wolfe, Linnie Marsh, ed. *John of the Mountains: The Unpublished Journals of John Muir.* Boston: Houghton Mifflin, 1938.

Woodcock, George. "The Lure of the Primitive." *American Scholar* 45 (Summer 1976):387–402.

Young, Samuel. *Alaska Days with John Muir.* New York: Fleming H. Revell, 1915.

Index